Praise for *Writing the Biographical Drama*

This book is a beautifully rendered journey into the joys, challenges, secrets, and time-tested methods of writing biographical dramas for the stage and cinema. Inspiring and wonderfully practical, this is *the* manual any writer, no matter the level of achievement, can turn to when wrestling with such questions as:

- How do I make my story relevant to today?
- What is the relationship between research and creativity?
- How much of myself can I pour into the life of this famous (or infamous) person?
- How do I explore a historical character's fatal flaws?

The book includes scores of examples derived from the work of such greats as Harold Pinter, David Mamet, David Hare, and Suzan-Lori Parks, but some of the best help comes from O'Neill's meticulous and eye-opening analysis of her own biographical dramas: about footballer Ron Barassi, landscape designer Edna Walling, and musician John Lennon. Her insights into crafting her own award-winning biographical dramas are treasures.

— **José Rivera**, *Academy Award nominated screenwriter of*
The Motorcycle Diaries *and Obie Award winning playwright*

Writing the Biographical drama deeply and precisely describes the dilemmas and opportunities of writing a biographical script for theater or screen. It sheds light on the hidden writing process and exposes it in a clear, practical way. Both playwrights and screenwriters will benefit from and be inspired by reading this book.

— **Motti Lerner**, *award-winning international playwright*
and screenwriter of Kastner *(1985),* Kapo in Jerusalem *(2016),*
and the feature film Spring 1941 *(2008)*

How to write from real life, from real events, and keep it truthful and vital and fascinating? This is a book we've been waiting for.

— **Patricia Cornelius**, *co-founder of Melbourne Workers Theatre*
and award-winning author of more than twenty plays, including
Slut *(2008),* The Call *(2009), and* Good, Do Not Go Gentle *(2010)*

Writing the **Biographical Drama**

An Essential Guide for Playwrights and Screenwriters

Writing the Biographical Drama

An Essential Guide for Playwrights and Screenwriters

Tee O'Neill (PhD)

upriver
PRESS

Published by Upriver Press
P. O. Box 51455
Colorado Springs, CO 80949
www.upriverpress.com

ISBN Paperback Version: 9798990623606
ISBN Ebook: 9798990623613

Library of Congress Control Number: 2025933950

First edition published as *Writing the Biodrama: Transforming Real Lives into Drama for Screen and Stage* in 2021 by Endeavor Literary Press.

Cover Design: James Clarke (jclarke.net)

Printed in the United States

Contents

Introduction

Films and plays based on real lives have been entertaining and enlightening audiences, wowing critics, and winning awards for centuries. Just think about *American Crime Story* and *Amadeus,* or *Bohemian Rhapsody* and *Brönte*, or *The Miracle Worker* and *The Motorcycle Diaries.*

Biographical dramas require a different approach to writing than fictional works. Unfortunately, there is a dearth of books on this topic to help aspiring screenwriters and playwrights. This book is designed to fill that void. It is a guide to researching, writing, and developing a dramatic story based on real people.

Drawing from my own experience as a playwright and lecturer of dramatic structure, and from my personal interviews with other prominent biographical drama writers, I outline every step of the writing process. These steps include choosing a suitable person; understanding the opportunities and pitfalls of biographical drama writing; researching; identifying the dramatic truth; structuring a story; developing a dramatic character; rewriting; and rehearsing.

Writing the Biographical Drama is designed primarily for screenwriters and playwrights, but novelists and documentary filmmakers who want to shape an engaging story based on a real person will also find it helpful. The book includes dozens of writing exercises, examples, and case studies to help you transform a biographical story into a powerful biographical drama that engages and delights audiences and readers.

The etymology of the word *playwright* implies that a drama writer is more akin to a shipwright or a wheelwright. Just as those workers build or repair ships and wheels, playwrights create and arrange dramatic works for the stage. Since the invention of cinema, we've called the more recent version of a playwright a *screenwriter.* The two professions are quite distinct; many playwrights never work as screenwriters and vice versa. But within both artistic professions are those who create biographical works about people from recent or historical eras. I shall call these writers *bio-dramatists.*

The work of bio-dramatists is challenging. Like all dramatists, writers of biographical scripts must get their screenplays or stage plays *right.* However, for the bio-dramatist, doing so includes more than just ensuring that the piece succeeds as a dramatic work. A biographical drama is not only about what the real-life subject did, like a documentary; rather, the final work will also reflect the bio-dramatist's portrayal of the story. Therefore, the writer must also have the right, both ethical and moral (and sometimes legal), to represent someone's life story. She or he must create a text based on what has been learned about the person's life and then imagine the work in such a way as to transform the facts into dramatic visual scenes for the audience and reader to experience. Therefore, the writer must fully absorb the biographical information and evaluate his or her own biases before generating dialogue, stage or screen directions, and scenes.

Bio-dramatists also face the challenge of research, which permeates the entire process of creation right up to the rehearsal phase. Research continues throughout the process because directors and actors need to navigate between the real person's story and the writer's dramatic creation.

This hard work is not likely to be in vain. Biographical dramas are the new rock-and-roll! People are endlessly interested in the lives of other humans. As a result, film and theater producers are eager to raise money to make biographical dramas about well-known people, in part because famous subjects have the crucial "brand-awareness factor" that draws public attention. Box office sales soar when biographical films that receive good reviews are released. Actors (and often writers) are garnished with or nominated for major awards for producing convincing portrayals of real people. I have written several biographical dramas for stage and screen, and one for a narrative concert. My experience demonstrates that when producers hear about or see a successful biographical drama they will pay the bio-dramatist to write more.

Knowing all of this, I found it surprising that nothing had been written specifically about writing biographical dramas. The lacuna came to my attention when I was commissioned to write a main stage play about a real-life sports legend. As I embarked on the project, I soon discovered that writing a script about a non-fictional character was quite different than writing a fictional script. When writing about fictional characters, I had freedom to invent as I wished—the characters existed only in my mind. Now, writing about a real person, I had to find a way to portray a character who existed independently of my imagination.

This distinction impacted the entire creative process. I faced new challenges in the research phase. I had to find a way to turn the messiness of actual life into a tight and compelling story. I had to be true to the facts while worrying about the audience's preconceptions of the subject. I questioned how my writing might make the subject's family and friends feel. I wondered how to compress the man's life into tight scenes while still being true to his story.

So, you will notice that my first biographical drama, a stage play titled *Barassi,* is mentioned a lot in the book. *Barassi* was a challenging, all-consuming project that got a lot of media attention, in part because it was about a well-loved and legendary Australian football player. The play had a highly successful first season and was nominated for a Premier's Literary Award. It was then transferred to a major arts center, followed by an interstate tour. Writing it forced me, for the first time, to solve problems and explore opportunities within the biographical drama genre. Much of what I learned became the basis of my PhD dissertation.

Barassi launched me into many other adventures in biographical drama writing. I'll share more about what I've learned throughout the book. It is, in fact, a reflection of my own life story—as a bio-dramatist and as a creative writing teacher for more than twenty years. These two aspects of my life are interconnected, enabling me to integrate theory and practice.

The book's first chapters provide an overview of biographical dramas—the profound reasons why audiences find them to be so powerful. Then I help you reflect on yourself as a writer; that is, to understand how your personal biases and agendas might influence your work. Next, an entire chapter gives you the opportunity learn from the firsthand experiences of numerous professional bio-dramatists. I then discuss the writer's ethics and responsibilities when writing about real people, and I address the criteria for choosing a suitable, compelling subject.

The latter chapters of the book deal with the process of researching, writing, and revising a script. You will read about dramatic structure, dialogue, character development, and timing. I present these topics not in a dry, academic way, but by analyzing many films and plays written by professional bio-dramatists.

The chapters conclude with writing exercises to help you research, shape, and develop your biographical drama. I hope those exercises help you apply what you learn. The best learning comes from transferring intellectual knowledge into practice. If you work through each chapter's exercises, you will learn much more than if you only read the book. You will be primed to do the hard *yakka* (yards) of writing and rewriting.

My suggestion is to read this book cover to cover and then try each writing exercise. Even the writing you do not use in the final draft will contribute to your final version. The exercises are designed to help you learn new writing skills and remind you about the stuff you already know!

Perhaps you already have an idea for a biographical drama script. I hope that what you learn from this book will kickstart your effort, helping you with all phases of imagining, researching, and writing. My aim is to help you breathe life into your biographical drama. May you find a creative way to translate a real life into a compelling dramatic story.

 *Alongside this book, Tee O'Neill provides an immersive and supportive home-study course — a biodrama bootcamp — that guides you into finishing a full rough draft of your script.*

CHAPTER 1

The Power of Biographical Drama

Why do audiences find biographical dramas to be so powerful? If we can thoroughly understand the answers to that question, we will be better equipped to craft our plays and films. So, I begin the book by presenting the academic research and the viewpoints of professional dramatists about why biographical dramas work so well to impact hearts and minds.

Humans are curious, especially about the lives of famous people. The revenue generated by popular magazine sales demonstrates that fact. We also enjoy true stories about less famous people who have lived extraordinary lives or have been through a life-changing incident, which is why so many books and movies have been made about them. Showing now at your cinema complex, or on your streaming device, or on your local stages, you can see biographical dramas about all sorts of people: musicians, politicians, royalty, a female jockey, and even a homeless African-American who tried to save his son from poverty.

Sir Ian McKellen, who has played many real people on stage and screen, believes audiences love biographical dramas because of "that little bit of thrill that they are getting close to an iconic or famous person whom they will never have a chance of meeting" (Cantrell and Luckhurst, 2010). Audiences love to see a biography *performed,* to see a character come alive in front of them.

However, our curiosity about people and this "little bit of thrill" only partially explain the huge popularity of biographical dramas. Psychologist Raymond Mar from York University found in his study a large overlap in the brain networks we use to understand stories and to understand the thoughts and feelings of others. Therefore, stories about people exercise our social cognitive abilities (March, 2018). Our need to create stories, to utilize our imaginations, goes back to primitive times when that noise in the bush might have been the wind or birds, or a saber tooth tiger!

We also like biographical dramas because they can encourage us to grow as human beings. Watching how other people go through difficult or challenging events can inspire us to live boldly and wisely. Stories allow us to engage in dangerous experiences without having to go through the actual pain. We can witness on stage or on screen the events that actually happened. By reenacting the emotional events that a real person experienced, biographical dramas reveal aspects of human life that can't be gleaned by reading a biography. Biographical dramas allow audiences to *witness* the character's experiences and emotions.

Biographical dramas can also unveil broader truths about life, the story behind the story that conveys a moral principle. For example, *The Assassination of Gianni Versace: An American Crime Story* (2018) has a lot to say about homosexuality and closeting in America. *Feud: Bette and Joan* (2017) reveals the stress women face to contort their images and personalities to compete for the spotlight. *The Lehman Trilogy* (2012) helps us contemplate the rise and fall of the American dream. *Official Secrets* (2019) explores the dangers of unchecked government power and of whistleblowing. Biographical dramas do more than just reenact factual events; they portray true stories in ways that deeply move the minds and hearts of audiences.

Therefore, your subject's story must be meaningful to your viewers, addressing what it means to be a human being. You'll need to reveal the universal interest that your character illustrates. To connect your subject's life and your audience's desire for meaning, you, as the writer, will need to dive deep into the heart and mind of your subject. You'll need to discover your subject's personal history, driving passions, psychological wiring, inner struggles, relational traits, flaws and weaknesses, qualities and strengths. Then you'll need to use this material to shape your drama.

Examples of Powerful Biographical Dramas

Let's take a closer look at some successful biographical dramas and discuss what makes them so compelling.

My biographical drama about Australian footballer Ron Barassi was about a successful celebrity sportsman. However, after researching his life and transforming his story into a drama, my play became a ghost story about Barassi's need to live up to his dead war-hero father. The play explored the darker side of blind ambition.

My second biographical drama, about Edna Walling, a famous horticulturist, showed how the work of renewing a neglected garden could restore a battered spirit. My research on Walling first uncovered her visionary achievements as a gardener and writer, but as I explored her life, I discovered that she had to contort many of her passions in order to be accepted in a male-dominated, conservative society. I wanted my script to reflect her struggle, disappointments, loneliness, and achievements. By dramatizing how her professional vision and love life had been thwarted, I was able to portray the haunting sadness of her life, and what it might have been had she received more support. The biographical drama also showed how Walling's artistic vision, which she realized by overcoming huge obstacles, now lives in many of Australia's backyards, patios, and balconies. Her story became a biographical drama that celebrates the human spirit, our ability to thrive despite neglect. After the play, audiences go home to nurture their gardens and plants, and to nurture themselves.

My narrative concert about former Beatle John Lennon was about the difference between having a child while young and having a child during middle age. My research revealed that Lennon, at age forty, had reached a point in life in which he was more reflective, and therefore in a much better position to be a father to his second son, Sean. He had abandoned his pursuit of constant attention and fevered drug use. Now he was approaching a (albeit edgy) happiness in domesticity. He had overcome demons that many of us will never face. Then he was shot dead in a street near his New York apartment. My script reveals Lennon's fascinating mind still rich with insights, which was reflected in his songwriting of that time. It also demonstrates what the world lost in 1980.

Bohemian Rhapsody (2018) is a screenplay by Andrew McCarten about an individual pursuing a dream with heroic intensity. It is also a family saga, the family being Freddie Mercury's band Queen. The biographical drama tackles how this bisexual British immigrant was nurtured, constrained, betrayed, forgiven, and reunited with his family. It is a prodigal son story. Interestingly, the writer's research consisted of "mainly talking to the band." As a result, much of the film presents the viewpoints of the surviving members of Queen (McDonald, 2017). The drama shows us how confused Mercury felt about love and ambition in a world that wanted rock stars to be white, straight-toothed, and heterosexual. The script shows how he responded to these obstacles, exceeding expectations by creating his unmistakable, eclectic sound.

Another powerful biographical drama is *Can You Ever Forgive Me?* (2018) by Lee Israel. This work is about a penniless, grumpy biographer who struggles to pay the vet bill for her much-loved cat. She stumbles on a way to make money by forging letters from successful dead writers. The script's power derives from the tension between the protagonist's drive to make money and her inner longing to write original works loved by everyone. This struggle makes the audience identify with (and root for) an unlikeable con woman.

The same cannot be said about audience responses to *Vice* (2018). The protagonist, former US Vice President Dick Cheney, remains unlikeable (even terrifying) in this screenplay by Adam McKay. The film shows how one man turned the normally bland job of vice president into a position of great power. In the film, Cheney changes the world forever (not for the better). The film has been praised, but many people criticized McKay for his dramatic interpretation of some facts. For example, McKay invented Cheney and his wife quoting Shakespeare during pillow talk, which, incidentally, was my favorite scene. With some clever cinematic devices, the film explained how the United States had rushed to war with Iraq. It left me feeling how vulnerable the world can be to unchecked ambition.

Cheney, a modern-day Macbeth, begins with good intentions. Like Macbeth, when fueled by a demanding wife and a Machiavellian mentor, he lost his principles. The drama gives audiences a real-life modern look into the common Shakespearian theme that power corrupts and that absolute power corrupts absolutely.

Similar themes abide in *Official Secrets* (2019), a film in which the central character puts her life, liberty, and marriage on the line for a cause. It traces her oscillating desire to not ignore a memo, which clearly shows that governments had been misusing power to go to war in Iraq. This script stayed close to the facts and provided a wonderful career-high role for Keira Knightly.

One of the best biographical films and plays ever, in my view, is also a personal favorite. *Amadeus* (1980), by Peter Shaffer, is about the relationship between two composers: Mozart, who is brilliant but has inappropriate manners, and Salieri, who is mediocre but has acceptable court tastes. The film dives into the heart of Salieri's agonizing jealousy as he confronts his mediocrity. It also displays Salieri's drive to destroy Mozart as something more than jealousy: a dramatic internal battle with God. Shaffer stretched the facts in order to tell the story, but I didn't mind that he threw historical accuracy out the window because the film is so engaging!

The Queen (2006), by Peter Morgan, explores British Queen Elizabeth's dealing with the death of her difficult daughter-in-law, Princess Diana. The events and people involved are in living memory, so Morgan did not have the liberty to play with history like Shaffer did. But he imagined Queen Elizabeth's private anguish, making it believable and relatable. The story's power derives from the way it domesticates the Queen of England. Morgan uses a common family problem (how to deal with divorced family members) to make imminently relatable a woman with whom most people have little in common.

Avalanche (2018), a play by Julia Leigh, is about the author and her new husband's journey into invitro fertilization (IVF). The play is about an ordinary middle-class couple going through recurring failure with IVF and the devastation it brings upon them. It dramatizes the dark side of a popular and expensive medical procedure that often does not work.

Summary

Audiences love to "witness" real-life experiences. They receive a thrill as the biographical drama leads them vicariously through a person's life while they contemplate ethical dilemmas, learn to overcome hardships, and discover ways to become better human beings. As you write your biographical drama, seek ways to connect audiences with these powerful attributes and focus on developing a profound theme that will impact your audience.

Biographical dramas can explore any human experience. From down-and-out writers to suburban couples to the Queen of England, biographical dramas tell real stories excavated from history. The bio-dramatist's call is to shape those stories into works of art, turning a life into great drama.

Biographical dramas create powerful dramatic roles for actors. We will address this aspect of writing in a later chapter, but as you consider your script, keep in mind that a successful script must inspire the actors. A well-written bio-drama, therefore, is an opportunity to attract top directors and actors who are keen to carry your blueprint into a performance.

Writing Exercises

1) *Learn from biographical dramas.* Watch again several biographical dramas that you have loved or loathed. Then ask: What were they *really* about, beyond the biography? What decisions did the writer make to shape the subject's life into a drama that conveys a broader truth. What engaged you and why? What did not engage you and why? (You can learn a lot from biographical dramas that, in your view, failed.) If you admire a film or play, think about what makes you feel that way. Those reasons can guide you in a positive direction as you write your script.

2) *Cast your biographical drama.* A powerful biographical drama will attract powerful actors. This exercise is for fun, but it can remind you to write for performance actors. Dream about who might work as your lead actor or actress. For instance, I imagined American (deceased) actress Katherine Hepburn as the best person to play Edna Walling. I occasionally kept Hepburn in my mind's eye as I developed my script, which helped me concentrate on the performability of my scenes. As I wrote, I imagined Edna and Katherine strolling across the gardens and telling off Walling's clients. I tacked two pictures of Edna and Katherine to the wall behind my computer to keep me inspired. (Both Hepburn and Walling would only expect the best from me!)

3) *The elevator pitch.* To discover your biographical focus, write an elevator speech, which is often called a *pitch*. Pretend you are in an elevator with a producer or director and then write down how

you would describe: (a) the most compelling aspect of your subject, and (b) why audiences would want to witness this person's story. You want to seduce your audience into being as interested in the story as you are. It is helpful to do this exercise in different draft stages of your biographical drama.

CHAPTER 2

Your Perspectives, Responsibilities, and Ethics

Biographical drama writers have many things in common with journalists and nonfiction writers. They all portray actual events and people, which requires extensive research. They make editorial decisions about what to leave in the story and what to exclude. They all need to think about how to tell a true story well, in a way that is meaningful and powerful. They also must consider ethical questions about the potential impact of their writing.

Despite efforts to be objective, writing biographical dramas, nonfiction books, and newspaper articles inescapably involves the viewpoints and prejudices of the writer. This does not mean the final work will be fake; rather, it means that the story will be influenced by the writer. So, bio-dramatists would do well to carefully consider how their own agendas, political positions, passions, personal histories, and ethical guidelines might influence the writing process.

This chapter is designed to help you think carefully about yourself as a writer in relation to the subject of your biographical drama. We'll address some important questions. For example, if you harbor animosity—or extreme admiration—for the lead character, will that sentiment sway your presentation of the facts? Is there anything in your background that might make it too emotionally painful to write about your subject, or would that emotional tension make your script stronger? Have you thought about your ethical framework regarding how the biographical drama might impact people in the story?

"Every writer needs to maintain an intense awareness of the world, especially of humanity's recurrent questions," said Sam Smiley, a screenwriter and playwriting teacher. "Why do people suffer? What is the meaning of death? Where do human struggles lead?" As writers grapple with these questions, Smiley believes they hone their perspectives on the world and their attitudes about human existence. The writer's perspective, he adds, "dictates the sorts of action most appropriate for that writer's drama" (Smiley, 2005).

In other words, the writer's viewpoints, values, beliefs, and experiences will unavoidably influence the outcome of any drama. But when writing a *biographical drama,* writers don't have the same freedoms that fiction writers have. They must find a way to express personal perspectives without inappropriately distorting the truth of the subject's life. Writers must widen their viewpoints to understand their time, culture, and attitude—and be curious about how their subjects understood their own time and culture. Writers must be cognizant of how their perspectives will shape the biographical drama.

Consider Your Passions and Interests

Central to writing well about a real person is sustained enthusiasm about the subject's character and life. The research and writing process is a long journey with the subject. So, if *you* are fascinated with the subject, then your audience will likely respond positively to your biographical drama.

While researching for *Barassi,* I took note of when my attention waxed and waned. For example, while I scanned Barassi's sporting achievements, I lingered on his social situation because I strongly wanted to know what type of man he was off the field as well as on the field. In my work about Edna Walling, I was always curious about the fights she had about gardens with her clients. Clearly, I enjoy drama! In both cases, my preferences and interests affected how I shaped the scripts.

Your preestablished passions and interests will greatly influence what you pursue during the research phase. Screenwriter David Seidler's strong curiosity resulted in *The King's Speech* (2010). He no doubt knew that Queen Elizabeth's father was the reluctant King George VI, who became king due to his brother's famous abdication. Seidler discovered a passing, but intriguing, remark about King George's stutter. Curiosity compelled Seidler to delve into the issue. He discovered that George's stutter was severe and that he couldn't overcome the problem until he met an unqualified speech therapist from Australia. (Several years later, Geoffrey Rush won a British Academy Film Award for his portrayal of that speech therapist.)

The film *Monster* (2003) emerged from screenwriter Patricia Lea Jenkins's curiosity about America's worst female serial rapist. After reading the tender letters she wrote from jail, Jenkins uncovered a powerful love story that influenced the film's outcome.

Intense curiosity about a person might link you to an important theme in your own life. I felt that I was the right person to tell Barassi's story, in part because I had played a lot of football as a young person. During my research, I found a deeper connection to Barassi, a strong need to understand the joy and pain that came from his relentless ambition. His difficulties and tenacity resonated with my own. Curiosity inspired me to examine the light and dark side of ambition. I've found that my experiences have influenced my curiosity about my dramatic subjects.

Sometimes I am asked to write a biographical drama only to find that I have no interest in the subject. Producers once asked me to write a biographical show about a successful North American singer/songwriter who was murdered in 1964. The story seemed dramatic, but after reading two biographies, listening to songs, and watching documentaries about the singer, I couldn't find a structure or a driving question that excited me. His problems didn't make me curious. I lacked the enthusiasm needed to commit a year of my life to shaping his story into a biographical drama.

The Autobiographical Impulse

Many bio-dramatists are drawn to the dramatic potential of a character because they identify with something deep in that person's life. This connection gives the writer a strong starting point to write. American playwright John Logan became obsessed with the red, maroon, and black paintings that Mark Rothko had been commissioned to create in 1958 for the Four Seasons restaurant at the landmark Seagram Building in New York. Rothko initially accepted the lucrative commission, but he ultimately withdrew his paintings and returned the money. Then, in 1970, he donated nine paintings to Tate Modern, the famed art gallery in London, just months before his suicide. The Seagram murals became the basis for *Red* (2009), a two-character drama about Rothko and his imagined assistant, Ken. Logan stated why he was drawn to writing a play about Rothko: "I always seek out those characters who simultaneously confuse me and vex me and challenge me and annoy me and inspire me. Rothko was one of those guys who fascinated me deeply" (Wallenberg, 2012).

Logan admits that the most compelling aspect was an autobiographical impulse: ". . . to me, it was mostly a play about my father. That's what was most compelling to me. What does a mentor give to a protégé, how does a father teach a son, and how do those power relationships shift?" (Ibid).

Similarly, playwright Roy Williams's difficult relationship with his father gave him the confidence to tackle a play about Marvin Gaye, the musician who was murdered by his own father. "We all have complicated relationships with our parents, and I hope those things can make the play quite universal," said Williams (personal interview, 2016).

Kenneth Lin also acknowledged an autobiographical impulse in the biographical play *Intelligence Slave* (2010), which is about a Holocaust survivor who was kept alive by the Nazis for possible usefulness. Lin saw a parallel in his own life as a Chinese-American playwright:

> I think that when you're a minority living in the United States of America, you don't have a great sense that you belong here, or that people fundamentally respect your humanity. Oftentimes, whatever rooms you're allowed to go into, you're allowed to go in there because you have some kind of a skill, and I saw that resonated with me and I wanted to write about that (personal interview, 2016).

The autobiographical impulse channels the writer's empathy,

the ability to understand another person's mental state and motivations. The writer finds a strong emotional alignment to the subject's story. These empathetic skills are akin to the work of actors, as affirmed by Motti Lerner.

> After a certain amount of external detail, you gradually, slowly get empathy with the character. This empathy is the medium, the instrument to explore his inner life—the same as an actor works. As I gather the biographical information, I develop an instinct, I develop insights for this inner life. I feel him in my heart. I feel him in my body—it is an association that is completely subjective—the same as an actor works (personal interview, 2016).

Actors think deeply about the motivations, beliefs, and value systems of the characters they portray. They must make those aspects of the characters come alive. To do this, some actors use "method acting" to identify as closely as possible with the character. They draw from the character's personal experiences.

Constantine Stanislavski pioneered a system of method acting that involves emotional memory. He writes: "The roles for which you haven't the appropriate feelings are those you will never play well" (Stanislavski, 1936). Having "appropriate feelings" for characters is also useful for biographical drama writers because acting and biographical scriptwriting are interpretative, empathetic, and imaginative types of work.

As a striking example of how a writer's personal experiences influence the creative process, consider playwright Bertolt Brecht's rewriting of *The Life of Galileo*. Brecht revised the play several times to better portray the dramatic historical events that the author had lived through, including the rise of Nazism, World War II, the nuclear age, and the partition of his native Germany. Dramatists such as Brecht present plays that are openly influenced by their social positions.

Brecht began writing *The Life of Galileo* in 1938. His experiences influenced the way he portrayed his protagonist's motivations. In the first version of the play, Brecht's philosopher-astronomer Galileo Galilei publicly misleads the Catholic Church and its inquisitors in order to secretly continue his work. As Brecht's editor, Eric Bentley, pointed out in the English version of the play's introduction, writers in 1930s fascist Germany knew that "truth had to be hidden" (Bentley, 1966). The second version of the play was performed in Los Angeles in 1947, after Brecht had fled from Hitler's Germany. After the atomic bombs had been dropped on Hiroshima and Nagasaki, he rewrote the play to be about a man who renounced his life's work and is ashamed of his cowardice. Brecht shared how the atomic destruction in 1945 influenced his work on Galileo, which he developed with actor Charles Laughton. "The atomic age made its debut at Hiroshima in the middle of our work. Overnight the biography of the founder of the new system of physics read differently" (Ibid).

By the time the play reached New York later that year, Brecht had faced an inquisition-like hearing conducted by the House Un-American Activities Committee (HUAC) in Washington, DC. A day after giving testimony, he left the US forever and returned to Germany, where he produced an even bleaker version of the play. Now simply called *Galileo,* it premiered in Cologne in 1955, five months after his death. Brecht's development of *Galileo* indicates that the nature of a biographical drama depends on how the author shapes it. The writer is often influenced by political and social experiences.

Arthur Miller, who lived in similarly interesting times, was also called to appear before the HUAC. Like Brecht, that experience influenced his dramaturgical decisions in writing *The Crucible* in 1953. In an interview with *The New Yorker* in 1996, Miller reflected on how he struggled to write a play explicitly about the events in his life and his country without being labelled a communist. *The Crucible* was a response to his circumstances.

Miller had read Charles W. Upham's 1867 two-volume study of the 1692 Salem witch trials, which described the personal relationships behind the trials. The events in 1692 resonated with what he was going through in 1952. Miller went to Salem to research what had occurred. He wrote scenes that reconstructed the relationship between John and Elizabeth Proctor and Abigail Williams, who would become the central characters in *The Crucible*. Miller revealed that he identified with adulterer John Proctor who, despite having a flawed character, stood up to the injustice of the Salem court (Miller, 1995). Miller invented a sexual relationship between John Proctor and Abigail, the servant who falsely accused John's wife of witchcraft. Miller himself married his long-term mistress, movie star Marilyn Monroe, in 1956.

Miller and Brecht, like their predecessors Shakespeare, Schiller, and Shaw, used dramatic license to shape the way people viewed history and historical characters. Miller's strategy was to draw parallels between the ignorance and hysteria he saw in the US and the Salem witch trials. In his preface to the published script, Miller wrote about the historical accuracy of the play. "This play is not history in the sense in which the word is used by the academic historian. . . . However, I believe the reader will discover there the essential nature of one of the strangest and most awful chapters in human history" (Ibid).

Miller seemed to want to confront audiences with the "then" and "now" of American society, to enable people to draw parallels between the literal Salem witch hunts and the methods of Senator John McCarthy in the early 1950s to identify and prosecute communists. He perhaps incorporated his experience with adultery in the scenes with Abigail and Proctor, and he probably based his portrayal of the religious authorities in Salem on his encounters with the ludicrous HUAC. One of Miller's characters in the *The Crucible*, Hale, attempted to convince the protagonist, John Proctor, to confess to witchcraft rather than hang. This element of the plot was like Miller's experience with HUAC Chairman Francis Walter, who offered Miller freedom if he would allow Walter to pose for a photograph with Marilyn Monroe (Miller, 1995). Miller refused Walter's *quid pro quo*. As a result, Miller went to court where he was charged with contempt of Congress. In the play, the protagonist, Proctor, refused Hale's offer and was taken to the gallows.

Brecht and Miller used personal and biographical material as a springboard for conveying thematic and political concerns. They shaped their biographical dramas around the facts but filtered them through a personal lens. Indeed, these plays could be less about the historical subjects than the playwrights' cultural and personal perspectives.

The Writer's Personal Agendas

All stories, including biographical dramas, can push agendas. So, it is good to be aware of what you want to push!

Patricia Cornelius and Robert Reid, who have won numerous writing awards, had a strong sense of the sociopolitical subject matter they wanted to explore. That agenda, for them, had priority over biographical information.

The writers of *Vice* (2018) had a clear agenda. In their view, former Vice President Dick Cheney and his political party were part of a self-interested movement that disregarded future generations. Their film emphasized that perspective.

David Mamet wrote his film *Phil Spector* (2013) about an American record producer, musician, and songwriter who was jailed for second-degree murder. Mamet's film leaves audiences thinking that Spector would have had a fairer trial if he hadn't been so famously weird.

In the play *Christie in Love* (1969), bio-dramatist Howard Brenton wanted to show how biographies could push personal agendas. Likewise, Alan Bennet had actors step out of their roles to comment on the underlying agendas of *The Habit of Art* (2009), which is about poet W.H. Auden and English composer Benjamin Britten.

There are also bio-dramatists who deliberately push an agenda that could be at cross-purposes to the people they portray. First, David Hare. He was accused of advancing his personal agenda when he redesigned his fringe hit *Fanshen* (1976) for a bigger, mainstream audience. The book titled *Fanshen* (1966), by Marxist writer William

Hinton, is about events in a village during the Chinese Revolution. Hinton lived and worked with Chinese peasants in 1948. Although his book endorsed land reform, Hare's play was critical of the practice. Hare wrote the following in his memoir: "He [Hinton] had discerned, quite correctly, that the play was indeed not saying the same thing as his book" (Hare, 2015). Hinton was aware that Hare's adaptation of his book had become widely popular and that it had been filmed by the BBC. So, he demanded "110 specific changes" be made to the play's text (Ibid). In negotiation with Hinton, Hare conceded to many of Hinton's requests. Hinton was a witness to the real events in China. He had gone through a long legal battle to force US customs officials to return his seized notes. So, Hare agreed on moral grounds to align his drama more closely with Hinton's version.

As you can see, a writer's personal agendas can influence biographical dramas in ways that sometimes conflict with the subject's reality. Bio-dramatists want audiences to believe the stories they tell, and storytellers are most convincing when they can change minds and reputations. But there is a line between dramatic interpretation and factual truth.

Robin Benger, the director of *Nelson Mandela: The Life and Times,* is wary of writers who elevate the mythical status of a renowned subject to even higher ground. "Biography is a double-edged sword," he said, "and I fear it is more often used to inflate the powerful for political ends" (Ngangura, 2017). Doing a thorough personal-awareness check of potential hidden agendas is crucial for your drama to be an authentic examination of a life story.

The Writer's Ethics

This leads me to question how writers should consider morality and ethics. Bio-dramatists can affect reputations and have an ongoing impact on living people. They have a lot of power over someone else's history. The writer's ethical stance will influence how she or he represents the facts of a subject's life.

Peter Morgan, the scriptwriter of *Frost/Nixon*, *The Queen*, *The Crown*, and *The Damned United*, said:

> . . . you either care about the repercussions of your writing or you don't. You're either a person with a conscience or you're not. I think I've got quite a fine conscience. There were a couple of things I lost sleep over with the play *Frost/Nixon*, so I went back and addressed them a bit more in the film (Morgan, 2009).

Indeed, dramatic presentations can alter public perceptions of real subjects and events, shifting views from positive to negative. Who will look at Facebook founder Mark Zuckerberg the same after viewing *The Social Network* (2010)?

The public view of British King Richard III was distorted by Shakespeare's famous representation of him as a hunchback megalomaniac who killed, among others, Prince Edward and Prince Richard in order to secure his position as king. This distortion influenced Josephine Tey as she wrote her bestselling 1951 novel *The Daughter of Time*. In that book, Tey challenged Shakespeare's earlier representation of the king by uncovering verifiable facts that showed Richard III could not have killed the two princes in the tower. Tey used fiction to reveal her findings, but nonfiction historian Robert

McCrum affirmed that Sir Thomas More's biography *The History of Richard III*, written between 1513 and 1518, initiated and spread a negative view of the English king.

> It was More's Richard that caught Shakespeare's eye and the version he put on stage, in his stunningly theatrical characterization of the 'poisonous hunchbacked toad.' The young Shakespeare reveled in his dramatic powers, and an ordinary chronicle play intended as routine propaganda became a star vehicle for a great actor, initially Richard Burbage. It was also Shakespeare's genius that transformed the king into a sinister comic performer, a character that audiences love and loathe. There is, however, no mistaking the playwright's loyalties. This is the victor's history, a version of events calculated to legitimize the reign of the founding Tudor, Henry VII (McCrum, 2012).

The combination of strong dramatic writing, great acting, and political bias affected the king's reputation for centuries. According to the Royal Shakespeare Company, *Richard III* is one of Shakespeare's most performed works worldwide.

The biographical material offered to Shakespeare seems to have been compelling, but one must not emphasize literary influences over creative inspiration. Historian Paul Kendall believes that Shakespeare did not create an unlikeable character just to please the monarchy; he was also in competition with fellow playwright Christopher Marlowe, who had recently written a hit titled *The Jew of Malta* (1590). Kendall believes that Shakespeare was motivated to create his own version of the murderous Barabbas when he wrote Richard's character (Kendall, 1955).

Major character revisionism did not stop in the Elizabethan era. Poor old Mozart and court composer Antonio Salieri had their reputations battered by Peter Shaffer's enduring film and play *Amadeus* (1980). Contrary to Shaffer's portrayal, Salieri was neither a bad composer nor a murderer. He was in fact an influential teacher with pupils such as Mozart's son and Franz Schubert. Mozart's untimely death was the result of rheumatic fever, not poison (Brown, 1992). Bio-dramatist Peter Arnott thinks that Shaffer sacrificed the truth and Salieri's reputation mainly for popular appeal.

> *Amadeus* had a much bigger impact on Salieri's reputation than Mozart's. It's all made up. Salieri didn't do it! He [Salieri] taught Beethoven how the play the piano. Showbiz is Darwinian. And Mozart is showbiz. If the price of creating this Mozart figure is to trash Salieri then so be it! . . . But that's not my ethos (personal interview, 2016).

This need to write a popular work based on attention-grabbing gossip might also motivate you. But be aware of the consequences of deliberately, or even accidently, portraying negative aspects of your subject that never happened. Embellishment of past events can have lasting effects. If the person is alive, you could also be sued for defamation.

Arnott goes on to say that he "still feels bad" about "carelessly" making a minor character Catholic when the character was Protestant in religion-sensitive Glasgow. An upset nephew of the minor character confronted Arnott after seeing the play. As Arnott explained, whether you were Catholic or Protestant in divided Glasgow was important.

Similarly, I also still feel bad about a scene in *Barassi* in which his coach, Norm Smith, calls the young footballer Hassa Mann a yellowbelly (coward). I had sourced this information from a biography about Smith. Mann, who was known as a brave player, saw the play and was allegedly upset. He told a third person that the scene never happened. The scene was meant to display Smith's volatility, not to be an accurate description of the young player he was unfairly berating. I still feel uncomfortable about that dialogue.

As you can see, your portrayal, whether accurate or not, can hurt the subject of your biographical drama and the subject's friends and relatives. You should carefully consider feelings and reputations as you construct your biographical drama.

Patricia Cornelius, author of *Savages* (2014), which won the Louis Esson Drama Award, was so mindful of protecting a central subject that she left her out of the play. *Savages* was inspired by Diane Brimble's death on a cruise ship. A 2010 investigation of her death found that Brimble had been drugged and then used for the sexual gratification of eight men. Instead of focusing on Brimble, Cornelius wrote her play about the men who had sex with her and who did not protect her when she overdosed. She had this to say about her choice to leave Brimble out:

> Someone wrote a naturalistic play about Brimble, about what happened, and it hurt her family and I did not want to hurt her. I did a lot of research and investigated the men. What attracted me to the case was the level of misogyny of these men who believed they could do all sorts of things to her body. The question driving the play was what gave these eight men license to behave so appallingly? Because I wanted to protect her, I didn't want her in the play (personal interview, 2016).

In the process of wanting to protect her subject, Cornelius found a pathway to write the tragic story.

Peter Arnott's ethics also guided him as he wrote his play about rock singer Janice Joplin. He said:

> I think that presenting herself 'on her own' is none of my business. What I want to look at is the way she presents herself in different circumstances—at a press conference, on the phone to somebody in a business situation—but the constant is self-presentation. Janice herself would say publicly 'no-one likes me. I'm always on show. No-one is interested in the real me.' But the paradox is that was a presentation in itself. She was smart enough to know that that is a presentation as well. She was caught in the layers of her own irony (personal interview, 2016).

Arnott was not interested in speculating what Joplin was like offstage, so most of his drama was set at an onstage concert. The dialogue was inspired by the words the singer actually said.

Peter Morgan believes writers can bypass some ethical considerations by approaching a life story from an "oblique angle." He believes that if biography is too "head on" it becomes too difficult to play around with the facts. For this reason, he chose to tell his story of David Frost and Richard Nixon in *Frost/Nixon* (2009) through the limiting prism of four televised interviews. This approach gives the audience a lot of room to fill in narrative gaps (Morgan, 2009).

Setting your biographical drama from an outsider's point of view can bypass some ethical considerations. Audiences are aware from the outset that biographical dramas are presented from a particular angle or from one person's subjective memory. *My Week with Marilyn* (2011) was written from the perspective of an adoring young assistant who, in 1957, had to look after the biggest star in the world, Marilyn Monroe, during a tumultuous week of filming

The Prince and the Showgirl (1957). *Downfall* (2004) depicts the final ten days of Adolph Hitler's reign from the perspective of his secretary, Frau Traudl Junge.

The Risk of Upsetting or Pleasing People

Writing a biographical drama takes a lot of nerve. Basically, you are saying "this is what happened" when you can't know everything. It takes even more nerve to write a play about a living person or a recently deceased person. I felt a big burden of responsibility when I wrote *Barassi*. I had met my widely loved subject when he was in his early seventies. I received his blessing to write the play, but I soon realized that his memory was unreliable. A few months into writing the script he publicly announced that he had Alzheimer's. I knew that a stage show about his life would need to avoid upsetting the public who adored him.

When writing about a living person, you have to consider how your character's significant others might respond to your representation. However, you must not overly self-censor or exclude an important truth. Otherwise, you risk weakening the drama. Truth is, of course, always subjective. As a writer, you should recognize that your subject and his or her admirers may not like your presentation of the facts. The choices are ultimately yours to make in relation to your artistic purpose. How you choose often involves a tension between doing what your subject prefers or doing what's best for dramatic impact. The goal should be to write the most dramatic and truthful script you can.

When producer Ray Stark wanted to write a stage show based

on successful vaudeville comic and actress Fanny Brice, who also happened to be his mother-in-law, he had a lot of people to appease. The result, *Funny Girl* (1968), was a whitewash of the real story, but a huge ongoing hit. A successful revival of *Funny Girl* was shown on the West End in London.

Another successful film that did *not* appease its subject, but caused serious injury, was the portrayal of bank robber Johnny Wojtowicz (called Sonny Wortzik in the film) in *Dog Day Afternoon* (1975). The script portrays Sonny, who held up a bank, making a deal with the FBI that led to his partner's death. At the time of the film, the real Johnny Wojtowicz was in jail for that same robbery. However, he had never made a deal with the FBI. This fact didn't stop inmates, after seeing the film, from beating him badly. Biographical dramas *can* have a significant impact on a living person's identity.

Sometimes bio-dramatists encounter conflicting views about the subject, making it difficult or impossible to avoid hurting someone. British playwright Roy Williams, when he researched and wrote his first biographical play titled *Soul* (2016), saw the possibility of causing harm to the memory of Marvin Gaye, who had been murdered in 1984. He said he felt a heavy burden while writing about such a gifted, widely loved musician who died in terrible circumstances.

Williams discovered that Gaye's siblings, Jeanne and Zeolla, had different opinions about their brother. These contradictory research findings, however, proved to be a helpful solution to staging the play. After interviewing Gaye's sisters, Williams turned them into disputatious narrators. In the play, they are reminiscent of a Greek chorus observing the Oedipal tragedy of Marvin's life (personal interview, 2016).

David Mamet also used contradictory research findings to help him write *Phil Spector* (2013). By including contradictions in the prosecuting evidence, he raised doubt about the real guilty verdict in Spector's case. He also left out the explanations for these contradictions in the finished film.

Bio-Dramatist As Whistleblower

Then there are cases in which the writer discovers painful truths about a subject. Depending on the writer's ethics and sense of social responsibility, he or she might become a whistleblower. Like all whistleblowers, that writer will face the costs of exposing uncomfortable truths. Doug Wright was, at first, attracted to writing a play about East German transvestite Charlotte von Mahlsdorf, whose bravery and fortitude helped her survive the Nazis and the Communists. As a gay man, Wright was in awe of Charlotte, a person who had survived so much hardship and yet seemed to thrive. However, his research later revealed that von Mahlsdorf had become a Stasi collaborator and might have been responsible for a gay friend's imprisonment. He comments:

> I couldn't hit upon a dramaturgical solution that would give a clean dramatic shape to the story of her life. It was too messy, too sprawling. I was infatuated with her and placed her on a pedestal. Then I saw her very human failings and felt betrayed and disillusioned. And finally, that morphed into a truer, more profound and adult love— the ability to view a person with all of their contradictions intact, and still recognize their fundamental value (Wright, 2006).

Wright's dramaturgical journey is another example of how the contradictions and difficulties in a subject's life can be a key to writing a richer play. Problems or ethical dilemmas that arise in the research might hold opportunities.

Upsetting Audiences with Your Creative License

The difficult choices involved in how to present painful *facts* about a subject are multiplied when making *creative* choices to improve dramatic impact. We will address the topic of creative license more thoroughly later in the book, but it is important to say here that the writer's use of creative license is directly connected to the writer's ethics.

While shaping his biographical drama *Lincoln* (2012), Tony Kushner did not realize that he would upset an entire state! Kushner had previously written an unflattering account of attorney Roy Cohn in his successful play and television drama *Angels in America: A Gay Fantasia on National Themes* (1993). In the foreword to the published text, he offered a disclaimer: "While artistic liberties were consciously taken to dramatize Cohn's presence, most of his characterization is actually based on fact" (Kushner, 1993). When he took similar "artistic liberties" in *Lincoln*, he was publicly questioned. Republican Congressman Joe Courtney, of Connecticut, wrote in an open letter that *Lincoln* wrongly portrayed two congressmen from his state as voting against the Thirteenth Amendment, which abolished slavery. In fact, all four of the state's representatives voted for the amendment in 1865. Courtney asked director Steven Spielberg to correct this error in the DVD version. Kushner responded to Courtney's criticisms with his own terse letter to the *The Wall Street Journal*: "In making changes to the voting sequence, we adhered to time-honored and completely legitimate standards for the creation of biographical drama. . . . I hope nobody is shocked to learn that I also made up dialogue and imagined encounters and invented characters" (Farley, 2013).

Kushner seemed annoyed, and perhaps surprised, that *Lincoln* was criticized. He had not considered the strong community feelings in Connecticut when creating his biographical drama. Kushner defended his screenplay with the same argument that any playwright could make about his or her work, but playwrights are seldom taken to task about historical accuracy the way screenwriters are. Perhaps that is because theater functions in smaller arenas than film.

Kushner's struggle with criticism and Peter Morgan's sleepless nights while writing *Frost/Nixon* demonstrate that representing real people on stage and screen can stir up difficult situations in the bio-dramatist's life.

How do other bio-dramatists cope with this pressure? When I asked that question to José Rivera, who wrote about revolutionary Che Guevara, he said he was very aware of Che's living relatives, fans, and enemies. But he eventually got down to business: "I don't lose sleep over it. I don't worry about it. Because I think what will happen is that a play like mine will be another voice in a larger conversation" (personal interview, 2016). Rivera's response is a refreshing and healthy approach. Bio-dramatists will never please everyone and they might be artistically thwarted if they try!

The risk of upsetting someone is much greater when the subject of a biographical drama is or was a divisive figure. It's simpler to write about someone who is universally deemed as evil, such as Pol Pot or Adolph Hitler, than it is to write about divisive figures, such as Margaret Thatcher or Donald Trump, who have eager supporters and angry detractors. Writing about political figures might touch a nerve because those people represent parties, nations, and ideologies.

Motti Lerner knew he would be touching some nerves with his play *Kastner*, but that pressure did not overly affect his creative process:

> I hope that this knowledge doesn't affect me too much. I'm trying my best to treat the characters and their plot as truthfully as possible, regardless of the public response. Although somewhere in the back of my mind I'm being cautious that if I'm attacked for something I wrote, I'll have the right answer. I don't think I'm writing plays to create a provocation. I'm writing about traumatic events because such events challenge the characters and force them to deal with fatal and existential questions. By exploring the trauma, I can discover more about the characters and about the context in which they had to take action (personal interview, 2016).

The possibility of being "attacked" when writing about a person is another good reason to make mindful decisions while writing. Ethical caution will help the bio-dramatist to withstand the criticism that will invariably come.

When I write, I'm aware that the people in my biographical dramas, and their relatives, could attend the shows. The most difficult criticism for me to accept is from my subjects and their friends and family. When the son of Barassi told me that his mother would "never make Dad a cut [sack] lunch," it hurt a bit. But theater and film work in images. A woman handing a man a cut lunch allowed me to show Barassi yet again rushing away from his home. The scene also revealed an increasingly perfunctory domestic relationship. My dramaturgical exigency only mildly upset my character's son, but it made me aware of how much I hoped to please him. If I had spoken to Barassi's son before opening night, would I have excluded the cut-lunch images? I have often wondered. If I had removed the scenes to assuage the son's feelings, the play probably would have been weaker.

Polly Teale had to work closely with Jean Rhys's granddaughter, Ellen, to maintain the rights of her play. She told me that she had a sense that "Ellen [was] on my shoulder." She didn't think that awareness affected her dramaturgical choices, but she was relieved that Ellen gave her the green light for the production (personal interview, 2016.)

Where will you stand on making art versus making people close to your subject happy?

Summary

It takes nerve to write a biographical drama because no biographical drama will please everyone. Confidence will strengthen when you are aware of your personal biases, agendas, responsibilities, and ethics. Ask yourself how sensitive you will be to the reputations of your subject and your subject's relational network. A good biographical drama has the power to change opinions, and your creativity is a license to thrill! Scripts that demonstrate a well-rounded view of the biography, but are also a rollicking good story tend to win over audiences (perhaps excluding relatives).

Writing Exercises

1) Think of a world leader you admire and another you dislike. Now imagine how you would tell each person's story. If I were to do this exercise based on former British Prime Minister Margaret Thatcher and Burmese human rights activist Aung San Su Kyi, my first instinct would be to portray Thatcher as a cold, handbag-wielding demagogue, a woman who had abandoned working class communities. Likewise, I would present Aung San Su Kyi as an articulate, passionate, and stylish freedom fighter who appealed to our better selves. My working class, humanist, and left-leaning roots would make it difficult for me to understand Thatcher or to criticize Aung San Su Kyi. However, a play about either of them would ultimately offer little if I didn't do the work to fully understand them with an open heart, a critical mind, objectivity, and interrogative vigor. Objectivity would help me recognize that middle-class people enjoyed lower taxes under Thatcher and that Aung San Su Kyi was accused of failing to protect the Rohinga refugees who were forced to flee Burma to Bangladesh. To write a biographical drama about each of these women, I would do well to talk to, or read about, the people who had been affected positively and negatively by both leaders.

2) What are your personal politics in relation to your subject? Should you check those sentiments at the door or let them drive your narrative? Spend some time free writing about that question.

3) What are your character's strongest views? Write a scene that

includes a short, imagined debate between your character and another character who defends the opposite viewpoint. You might not use this scene, but it will help you deepen your understanding of the issues that surround your character's life.

4) Write three scenes, first from your subject's point of view and then from an antagonist's perspective. Third, write the scene from an outsider's viewpoint. This exercise can deepen your understanding about the subject, and even surprise you.

CHAPTER 3

Learning from the Masters

As I prepared to write this book, I had the opportunity to hold interviews with numerous internationally renowned playwrights and screenwriters. This chapter will give you an opportunity to learn from some of those people. My goal here is not to address all the facets of writing a biographical drama; rather, I hope the summaries of my interviews with these dramatists will provide you with a helpful overview of their writing styles and methods. They are fascinating people with diverse approaches to the craft. I chose them because they practice both playwriting and screenwriting.

I was impressed by the generosity with which the writers shared their insights about writing biographical dramas. They talked about the importance of exhaustive research in order to gain a deep understanding of a character's history, personality, behavior, achievements, and failures. Nearly all of them said that writing a biographical drama enriched their lives.

José Rivera

I had the pleasure of talking with José Rivera on May 9, 2016. He is a Puerto Rican-born American playwright and screenwriter who twice won the Obie Award and who wrote an Academy Award nominated screenplay about Argentine revolutionary Che Guevara titled *The Motorcycle Diaries* (2004). He also wrote a full-length play titled *The School for the Americas* (2007), also about Guevara. As I wrote this book, he was writing the Netflix pilot of *One Hundred Years of Solitude*, the 1967 novel by Gabriel Garcia Márquez.

Rivera, who is soft-spoken and has the kindest smile, emphasized the importance of research. He likes to read everything he can find about his subjects, immersing himself in their lives before he begins to shape the narrative. He calls this approach "glutting" because he conducts research until it feels there is nothing left to find. Only then does he work on the script.

The problem with this approach, he told me, is that research can become a way of putting off the moment when you put pen to paper or fingers to keyboard. Indeed, Rivera warns that research can be "the best form of procrastination." To prevent delays, he always keeps a notebook close at hand so that he can jot down crucial ideas that arise from the research. This enables him to start writing early in the creative process.

A question that guides him is: Who would I be if I were this person? In his words: "I think part of writing is the act of self-transformation. So, you involve yourself in an issue and, you know, a metaphor or poetic world that you're trying to create, and I think you have to allow yourself to change into that and ask yourself what am I if I were this?"

From Rivera we learn that writing a biographical drama compels us to, metaphorically, walk in our subject's shoes. Rivera posed another provocative question: "Who would I be if I lived this person's life?"

Kenneth Lin

I met Kenneth Lin on May 8, 2016 in a tea shop near Ground Zero in New York City, where he had a short break from his job as a staff writer for the television series *House of Cards*. Lin is a deep thinker and hard worker. When we talked, he was under commission to write the staged story of Russian billionaire Mikhail Khordokovsky. My interview with him was perfect timing; he was deep into the creative process.

Lin placed a similar emphasis on exhaustive reading, especially if the subject was still alive. "So, so much of it was just reading, and reading, and reading, until I started being like 'Oh, now I understand. I understand what it means to be in this particular situation.'" When research gives him confidence that he deeply understands the subject, then he feels ready to start writing. He is drawn to characters like concentration camp survivor Kurt Hertzstark or jailed oligarch Mikhail Khodorkovksy because they have problems he wants to solve: "How do you love a world that doesn't love you back, or is always conspiring to kind of dehumanize you?" In this sense, he believes that biographical drama writers often write about their own lives, even though they are writing a biographical work. He has linked his characters to his life as a Chinese American, the experience of not being accepted by the mainstream in his country, but also not fitting in the immigrant culture. "You know, being thrown into these situations where you don't find a lot of yourself, and trying to make your way through."

Willie Russell

In November of 2016, I held an interview with Willie Russell in deep, dark Devon, in England's South West. He told me that his approach to biographical drama requires less research, or perhaps a different kind of research. A Liverpool playwright and screenwriter, Russell is a big bear of a man best known for his 1980 play and Academy Award nominated film *Educating Rita*. Early in his career he wrote *John, Paul, George, Ringo and . . . Bert* (1974) about The Beatles. He is also known for his biographical play, musical, and film script titled *Our Day Out* (1987), which was based on the colleagues he had when he was a teacher in Liverpool.

Russell told me that he eschewed research. He is much happier to "loot his own past," to write about people from his life and then "go through the process of imagination." This process might take many years, he said, adding that writers must allow the experience to sit inside and be "dredged up." He claimed that the product of this process is a "very accurate" portrayal of biographical characters. This approach fascinated me, but I would find it limiting to stick to people from my own history.

For *Educating Rita* (1983), Russell created one of my favorite characters: the marvelous Rita, a working-class hairdresser who defied the class system and got an Ivy League education. Russell "looted his past" when he created Rita's character. She was, in fact, based on the writer himself. Russell had been a hairdresser for women who also longed for an education. However, he told me that he did more research to write his musical about The Beatles; although he had seen them in concert, he didn't know them personally.

Motti Lerner

Motti Lerner is one of Israel's foremost playwrights and screenwriters. He has written many biographical dramas, including *Kastner* (1985) about a Jewish Hungarian journalist who helped Jews escape from occupied Europe during the Holocaust and who was later charged with collaborating with the Nazis. *The Murder of Isaac* (1999) is about the 1995 assassination of Israel's Prime Minister Yitzhak Rabin. *Paulus* (2013) is about Saint Paul.

Lerner and I keep running into each other at international festivals. He is a delightful conversationalist as well as the author of the important book titled *The Playwright's Purpose* (2015). My interview with him in August 2016 occurred over Skype while he was home in Tel Aviv. His primary interest in writing biographical dramas is to discover "the real story that hasn't been told." He seeks characters from recent and ancient history and then challenges himself to understand their motivations.

In other words, he believes the engine of a play is driven by the question of *why* the character did what he or she did. This is like Rivera's question: "Who would I be if I were this person?" The answer, of course, depends on discovering the character's driving motivations. Understanding these motivations enables the writer to animate the drama. This requires the "glutting" research that Rivera prefers. However, a certain amount of educated guessing is also needed.

When creating his play *Kastner,* Lerner began with a clear goal. The play is about a man who, Lerner believed, was wrongly accused of collaborating with the Nazis during World War II.

Leading the spectator into asking why the Israeli society has been so fundamentally wrong in its judgment of Kastner was certainly an important goal, but perhaps an even more important goal is to strengthen the spectator in his/her obligation of taking responsibility for his own faith and for the faith of the society he lives in—in a time of a catastrophe (personal interview, 2016).

Rudolph Israel Kastner had already been murdered when Israel's Supreme Court overturned most of the rulings that pertained to his alleged Nazi collaborations. Lerner's play told Kastner's story based on facts uncovered by his research. The play served, posthumously, to further vindicate Kastner.

I was excited to see how biographical dramas can restore a reputation. That could be an excellent motivation to help you write your biographical drama. Perhaps you can help right past wrongs.

Robert Reid

Talking with my long-time friend, playwright Robert Reid, is always illuminating . . . and exhausting. In August 2016, we talked nonstop for over four hours about his biographical dramas! Reid has written dozens of plays for fringe and mainstream companies, including *The Bill Hicks Story* for the Comedy Festival.

Reid revealed a completely different approach to his initial research. For Rivera, Lerner, and others, the primary task is to breathe life into the subject; to find a way, through research, to understand what drives the subject. By contrast, Reid turns that approach on its head. He told me that he obsesses over a theme that has fascinated him and "dogged" him. Emerging from that theme, a real subject comes to mind that fits his thematic goals. Reid, in other words, begins the process by knowing what kind of person he needs for his plays, and then he uses research to discover someone who fits the mold.

Polly Teale

I met with British writer and director Polly Teale in her South London home. She wrote two highly successful biographical plays: *Brontë* (2005), about the Brontë family, and *After Mrs. Rochester* (2003), a work about Jean Rhys that won an Evening Standard Theatre Award. She also wrote, with Linda Brogan, *Speechless* (2011), a play that dramatizes the lives of elective mute twins June and Jennifer Gibbons.

Teale, during her research, feels like a detective in a foreign land. She loves the process of studying photos, images, and objects related to her subject, and she often goes on field research trips. She believes that it's important to be at locations where the subject lived and visited—to touch, see, and smell the surroundings. This helps her elevate the subject's world in a sensual, visceral way. Teale, with a spirit of adventure, stays open to whatever might jump out and surprise her. She looks for what might help her understand the depth and texture of the subject's life. She seeks for clues about how to re-enact the person's life.

Beyond these physical, sensory elements, Teale is motivated by an Oscar Wilde quote: "One's real life is so often the life that one does not lead." I pondered this and sadly realized that this is true of many women and minorities.

After Teale finishes an immersive research phase, she said she embarks on a process of "mulching together all the gathered material." In her words:

> You've got all this material and you need to distill it to allow the world of the script into one entity. The subjects' lives need to be rooted in the time and place of history as well as the socio-cultural and economic and physical reality of their lives. But what draws me in is the human story, the complex inner world of the characters. As a writer, I desire to go beyond the surface, to their emotions, their imaginations, their memories, dreams, longings—all the stuff that goes along with living (personal interview, 2016).

Teale's productions are very physical. Her writing is fueled by a desire to go beyond naturalism and to discover the character's private world. She will write scenes in which the characters literally and physically enact whatever they secretly feel or imagine. She shows the social facade as a thin layer beneath which bubbles a river of suppressed emotion.

For example, during a scene in which two people share tea around a table, one character secretly feels irate toward the other. Suddenly, the audience sees hidden emotions erupt as an angry man viciously attacks the partner, who in turn crawls under the table. Then the angry man suppresses his emotions and returns to drinking tea. The audience discovers that below a social ritual, one man's burning anger could lead to a murder.

Roy Williams

Roy Williams is an Evening Standard Award-winning British playwright and screenwriter whose first biographical play is titled *Soul: The Untold Story of Marvin Gaye* (2016). I've known Roy for many years and have watched his career blossom with a fan's pleasure and an acquaintance's pride.

We met in the café of the Royal Court Theatre in Sloane Square. He told me that he didn't know much about Marvin Gaye when he was approached to write a play about the renowned musician. After he listened to Gaye's vast collection of recordings and read about his life, Williams saw a way into the story. Williams's father left for America when Williams was two. Their difficult relationship, said Williams, was pivotal in convincing him that he could relate to Gaye.

"Though nowhere near the same, the relationship that Marvin had with his father really resonated with me and that's one of the reasons I felt I could tell the story," said Williams. "I could get an aspect of that, and I realized then that audiences could. We all have complicated relationships with our parents, and I hope those things can make the play quite universal."

Finding that kind of personal connection with your subject is a powerful way to write a compelling biographical drama.

Patricia Cornelius

Patricia Cornelius is one of Australia's great playwrights. We met in the foyer of a theater in Melbourne where both of us have had our plays performed. She wrote the Australian Writer's Guild (AWGIE) award-winning play titled *Slut* (2008) and *Savages* (2013), both about women who, for a brief time, were in Australian media headlines.

Cornelius was inspired to write *Slut* when she saw how the Australian press treated a woman who had been assaulted. When a man came to help her, he was shot dead. The woman happened to be in a relationship with the shooter, who was in a motorcycle gang. Cornelius says: "The media talked about her as if she was complicit in the crime, and I was struck by how backward it was. Instead of calling her a slut, they called her a 'party girl,' the inference being that she asked for it."

This prompted Cornelius to write a play loosely based on the woman. It explores the notion that a woman who has a lively sex life might embrace the word *slut* only to be worn down by the label in the end. "It's a no-win situation to be a slut, no matter how much a girl thinks her life is her own and that she can do whatever she wants," Cornelius said.

Cornelius was also alarmed by hearing young people in her writing workshop refer to girls as sluts. So, she included in her play a chorus of young women who talk about the central character, Lolita. The young women discuss her life, chatting about Lolita's difficult and dangerous sexual relationships during her twenties. At the climax of the play, it is revealed that Lolita had been shot by her drug-addled biker boyfriend. The ending of the play resonates with Australians who are still horrified by a crime that occurred in a country known to be a safe place to live.

Nick Stimson

Nick is an associate director of The Theatre Royal Plymouth. His fascination with people has led to many biographical dramas, including about painters Beryl Cook and Stanley Spencer; English writers J.M. Barrie and Mary Shelley; suffragette Cristabel Pankhurt; and Polish children's author, humanitarian, and Holocaust victim Janusz Korczak. He is attracted to terrific biographic stories and the exciting ideas for vivid scenes that spring up from them. He feels it is important to find a truth inside biographical stories. "It's about digging down past the formal history to imagine what the real drive was." When he finds a truth that he "needs to tell," he feels safe to write the story. In his words:

> Yeah, I think that's it, isn't it? We know when we've reached the truth that we need to tell and we feel safe at that point. We feel OK. . . . It may not be an actual factual truth, but it's a truth that lies inside the piece. It's like when a painter knows, 'I'll stop now, I've done it' and if it annoys people, if it pisses people off, if they feel they need to walk out of the theater in protest, then so be it (personal interview, 2016).

Stimson wrote a musical titled *Korczak* about children's author and orphanage founder Janusz Korczak, who stayed with his children when they were taken to the Treblinka death camp. It was staged in the State Jewish Theatre in Warsaw before an audience of Holocaust survivors. Police with machine guns protected the theater. Stimson and his team had been warned that fascists could initiate a firebomb attack because of Stimson's play. He told me about the concern he had for the young people performing the biographical drama, adding that everyone involved thought the work was important to perform despite the risks. While writing the book and lyrics for the biographical drama, he had a profound sense that he was doing exactly what he was meant to do.

Rebecca Louise Miller

I met with Rebecca Louise Miller in a Brooklyn café in 2016 when she was deep into drafting her play *Capacity*, which is about Einstein's first wife, Mileva Maric. On top of the usual pressure to make sure each scene had a dramatic drive, she found she was not alone. Mileva was like a constant writing companion.

"It's not just me grinding into the keyboard," Miller said. "[Mileva] has been driven crazy by the fact that her story hasn't been told yet."

During research, Miller discovered that Mileva was yet another woman whose genius had been overlooked. Mileva "gave up her passion and lost everything and then there were little things that just made her feel like actor catnip to me, like the fact that she had a congenital hip deformity and a limp when she walked and could sing and could do all these things. She just stayed in my head and there was this weird resonance for me. I feel like I come from a long line of frustrated women."

Capacity enjoyed a sold-out and critically acclaimed run at Main Stage West in Sebastopol, CA in 2017. It was named one of the Bay Area's Top Ten Torn Tickets and received the only five-star review by local critic David Templeton during his two-decade career.

Peter Arnott

I met Peter Arnott at a mutual friend's house in North London. He was down from his hometown in Scotland to talk to BBC producers about a script. Arnott has written many biographical dramas, including works about singer Janice Joplin, boxer Benny Lynch, fighter pilot Lydia Litvyak, and assassin John Wilkes-Booth.

Arnott says his attraction to writing about real people comes down to being "terrible at making up stories." Arnott seeks to find "the tiny little human stories that are inside huge epic ones." For example, his play about the female fighter pilot who shot down eleven German planes in the battle of Stalingrad is, at its heart, a story about the struggles of women and about a woman fighting against Fascism. *White Rose* (1985) was remounted at the Traverse theater nearly thirty years after the original production, which starred Tilda Swinton and launched her brilliant acting career.

These experienced, dedicated writers showed me how seriously they take the job of creating a theatrical character based on the life of a real person. For them, research and writing biographical dramas is challenging, exhilarating, and even dangerous. They expect to learn something profound. They open their hearts and minds and then use their talents to discover the meaning and mystery of their subjects' lives.

Clearly bio-dramatists have more freedom to arrange facts in ways that increase drama, add excitement, and provide deeper insight. But with that freedom comes tremendous difficulty and risk. Purists might respond with disdain!

But there can be an even greater danger for the dramatist. José Rivera told me, "When *The Motorcycle Diaries* came out, the producers strongly suggested I get an unlisted number because they were certain that the right-wing Cuban community in Miami would literally come after me." Thankfully, Rivera told me, that never happened. But a conservative screenwriter was so appalled by Rivera's film that he told him, "You have blood on your hands."

It required guards with machine guns to protect the production crew of Nick Stimson's musical biographical drama about Janusz Korczak. I wondered whether the creative writing process would have changed if Stimson had known ahead of time that his work would cause so much risk. So I asked him. He answered, "No, I don't think it would have. I think *Korczak* was the only piece I've ever written that I actually felt like this is what I was meant to do."

The commitment to write biographical stories, despite difficulty and danger, was a primary, driving characteristic of these bio-dramatists.

Writing Exercises

1) *Find what resonates with you.* Some writers I interviewed spoke of needing to find a personal connection with their subjects. Finding that resonance between you and a subject can be a major first step toward understanding your character. It can add passion to the

writing process and provide a platform on which to build the script. What do you have in common with your character?

Roy Williams had a difficult relationship with his father, as did Marvin Gaye. Kenneth Lin felt like an outsider in his own country, as did the central character of his play *Intelligence Slave.* I shared with Barassi the agony of thwarted ambition. What aspects of your character's life do you deeply understand? Divorce, medical issues, body type, socioeconomic status. Some aspects may not be immediately obvious, so spend significant time in research.

2) *Commit to learning.* Biographical dramas must evoke enduring images and memories that you might not have experienced. What *don't* you have in common with your subject and how might you go about knowing what it must have been like to be that person?

I had never performed in front of one hundred thousand football fans, so I took a friend's kid to kick a footy at half-time during a big match at the Melbourne Cricket Ground. This experience gave me a physical sense of the noise and energy generated by a huge crowd.

Polly Teale had never lived as a woman in nineteenth century Yorkshire, so she visited modern Yorkshire and walked across the moors like the Brontë's. She did this while wearing the restrictive shoes worn by women in that era.

What interesting ways can you devise to find out what it was like to experience life the way your character did?

3) *Understand your subject's emotions.* Motti Lerner gathers biographical information and then finds insights into the subject's emotional life. Through research, Lerner gradually develops an

intimacy with his subject. Kenneth Lin immerses himself in research until he knows what it must have been like to be the subject. Rivera asks himself, *Who would I be if I were this person?* We will address research in a later chapter, but for now brainstorm the steps you could take to deeply understand your subject's emotional complexity.

CHAPTER 4

The Legality of It All

Playwrights and screenwriters, as they consider whether to write a biographical drama, often worry that they will run into a buzzsaw of complicated legal barriers. Such concerns are legitimate because biographical dramas are about real people (living or deceased) who might not want you to portray some aspects of their lives.

This chapter offers an overview of common legal frameworks pertaining to defamation, the right to privacy, copyright, and the use of artificial intelligence. It is not designed to be professional legal advice. Each country has its own laws and each creative work might involve unique factors that require a lawyer's counsel. That said, with some basic knowledge, writers can manage most legal worries without cost. By knowing which legal issues to consider early in the research and writing process, you can proceed with confidence.

Defamation and the Law

Defamation is a broad term. We all know that it refers to saying or writing something that might damage a person's reputation. In legal contexts, defamation is an umbrella term that covers both libel and slander. *Libel* refers to written content, such as a newspaper article, and *slander* pertains to verbal statements, such as content presented on the radio or television.

It is not automatically illegal to publish (in any format) negative facts about people. To be well-informed citizens, we need accurate reporting about politicians' negative behaviors and histories. So, in most democracies, the laws allow the press to publish facts about politicians and others even when that news will bring harm to the subject's reputation. News reporters, for example, can write or talk about people's crimes, affairs, mistakes, incompetencies, lies, and fraud. However, it is essential to ensure that negative reporting is A) factual and B) published without malicious intent.

"There is only one complete and unconditional defense to a civil action for libel: that the facts stated are [able to be verified]," according to *The Associated Press Stylebook*. "The important thing is to be able to satisfy a jury that the libelous statement is substantially correct."

Factual truth, therefore, is a strong source of protection against claims of libel and slander. The courts in most democracies give freedom to writers to publish negative information about people—if they handle the material responsibly. But legal protections can be lost or diluted if the author is negligent with the truth, and especially if the plaintiff can prove the author's negligence was driven by malicious intent. A reporter, for example, might make an innocent error when writing an article with libelous statements, but to win a case, the plaintiff would likely have to prove that the reporter *intended* to publish an untrue libelous statement with *malicious intent* to hurt the plaintiff's reputation.

It is interesting to look at the defamation case against the Netflix Emmy award-winning *Baby Reindeer* television series (2024), which was first presented as a stage play. The writer, Richard Gadd, worked as a bartender in London while pursuing a stand-up comedy career. During that time, he encountered a woman, Fiona Harvey, who, according to Gadd, began to stalk him. He based his award-winning play on his alleged interactions with Harvey. The play's success garnered the attention of Netflix, who invited him to write the television series.

Then the situation got murky. Netflix was sued because the company presented the series as a *true story* instead of saying that it was *based on* or *inspired by* true events. (Gadd's play did include that disclaimer.) The company claimed to have done everything possible to disguise the identity of the subjects in the series. For example, Gadd, who played himself in the series, changed Fiona's name to Martha Scott. Nevertheless, some legal experts considered these identity-disguising efforts to be thin. The plaintiff's case was more serious because the series portrayed her as having been convicted of a crime, which was not the case.

As reported in *The New York Times* (September 30, 2024), Lyrissa Lidsky, a law professor who is an expert in media law and defamation, cautioned that writers need to be careful with how they present biographical dramas. "When you're on notice that the source material you're adapting from has deviations from a true story and that you then make the choice to go back and portray it as truth, there is a chance your audience will believe it is true," Lidsky said. "And not just true about your fictional character, but true about the real character upon which the story is based."

Perhaps Gadd embellished the story to make a dramatic point—a common matter of artistic license—but Netflix could have reduced the risk of legal problems if they had presented the series with a simple disclaimer: "Based on true events" or "Inspired by true events." Gadd also could have avoided problems by including only verifiable facts about the subject in his script.

This legal debacle illustrates why playwrights and screenwriters should be cautious about writing anything defamatory about a person if those elements of the story cannot be verified. Changing characters' names or adding a disclaimer of "based on true events" can be helpful, but if your biographical drama includes unverifiable details that might harm the subjects' reputations, you would be wise to find a different approach or seek legal advice.

The Right to Privacy

In the US, the purpose of right-to-privacy laws was elegantly stated in a famous Supreme Court case. "The makers of our Constitution undertook to secure conditions favorable to the pursuit of happiness. . . . They conferred, as against the government, the right to be let alone—the most comprehensive of rights and the right most valued by civilized men" (*Olmstead vs. United States, 277 U.S. 438, 478*).

That is a valuable right for all of us. Nevertheless, most democracies allow film and theater writers to create a production about any living person without permission, if we adhere to right-to-privacy laws. These laws can differ from country to country. In general, you cannot reveal the private facts of someone's life (i.e., facts that are not publicly known) or intrude on someone's private space while writing your scripts. For example, if a subject was convicted of a crime, the writer can usually disclose facts that have been published in court records.

Most privacy law centers on the question of "public interest." The public interest principle usually protects information that is deemed to be important to the broader community. If a man running to be president of a country is reported to be having an extramarital affair, that would be a matter of public interest, but if a truck driver is accused of having an extramarital affair, the courts would likely deem that news to be private. The courts usually hold that information about famous individuals is in the public interest. It is difficult for playwrights and screenwriters to infringe on the privacy rights of famous people because so much has been written about them already.

You do not need permission from the subject to write a biographical drama. It is legal to write unauthorized biographies in any form, including books, plays, and films. Biographers often take the unauthorized route because they don't want the people in the story to constrain them. After all, the characters may be reluctant to discuss the most compelling dramatic details of the story, especially if those details are unseemly.

It can be helpful, however, to obtain permission from the subjects (if they are still alive), in part because the writer will usually want to interview them—to hear directly from "the horse's mouth." When interviewing your characters, you will need to learn as much as possible from them while also maintaining artistic independence. You need the freedom to decide how to write the story, even if that means including negative aspects of their lives.

I have found that most characters are excited to know that someone is producing a play or film about them. That attitude might change if they discover that you are including worrisome information about them in the script. I know from experience. Ron Barassi gave me wholehearted permission to write a stage play about his life. All was going well until he learned that the show would reveal some negative facts about him. I woke one morning to see an article in a major newspaper stating that Barassi, who was much loved by Australians, was upset and hoped that the show would be scrapped. This happened a week before the show's opening, which was a blow to our marketing campaign. But, after reading the great reviews about the production, Barassi came to a performance and then went on radio shows to rave about it.

Copyrights and Public Domain

Copyright laws are designed to protect intellectual property from theft and plagiarism. They are foundational in a democracy, and they allow creators to earn a living from their work. When conducting research for a biographical drama, you will need to respect the copyright protections of your source material.

Researchers and writers are allowed to gather facts and then convey that information in new ways. Historians do this all the time when writing books or making documentaries. However, writers are not allowed to simply "copy and paste" another person's creative work (poems, song lyrics, photographs, scripts, etc.). That would be plagiarism, the theft of another person's intellectual property.

There are exceptions to this rule, such as when source material has entered the "public domain." When a work is in public domain, the copyright has expired. According to legal experts at Stanford University Libraries, "the term *public domain* refers to creative materials that are not protected by intellectual property laws such as copyright, trademark, or patent laws. The public owns these works, not an individual author or artist. Anyone can use a public domain work without obtaining permission, but no one can ever own it." In these cases, you can adapt the original material without seeking formal permission or paying for the rights.

When do creative works enter the public domain? Again, the laws of each country will vary. According to a 2019 law in the US, works published before January 1, 1924 are usually in the public domain. However, if the work was published after 1977, the copyright will not expire until seventy years after the author's (or all authors) death.

Writers also need to be aware of "fair use" laws. According to *The Chicago Manual of Style*, fair use law "allows authors to quote from other authors' works or to reproduce small amounts of graphic or pictorial material for purposes of review or criticism or to illustrate or buttress their own points. Authors invoking fair use should transcribe accurately and give credit to their sources. They should not quote in such a way as to make the author of the quoted passage seem to be saying something opposite to, or different from, what was intended."

Again, be sure to check your own country's copyright laws, especially as they pertain to the use of poetry and song lyrics.

Content Generated by Artificial Intelligence

AI has been released upon us and there is no turning back. Many people believe this rapidly advancing technology is a danger to our industry, that generative AI will replace writers and lead to an outpouring of generic scripts that flood our world with "sludge."

Artificial intelligence is forcing courts to address new legal questions. One issue is whether works created by AI can have a copyright. At the time of this writing, US law says that only a human can hold a copyright. Thus, any text (or images and music) generated by AI cannot have copyright protection. The same is basically true in Australia, except that Australian law adds a layer of complexity by saying a work can have copyright protection if a human author has contributed substantial "independent intellectual effort." How much human effort is enough to give your work copyright protection? The line between human-generated text and AI-generated content is getting blurry.

Writers and publishers also must struggle with numerous ethical dilemmas surrounding generative AI. My own publisher (Upriver Press) has published a statement explaining why they reject the use of AI in book publishing. First, they say that AI companies "have stolen troves of copyrighted content, the hard work of journalists, authors, and publishers," to train their algorithms. "When companies blatantly disregard laws that protect intellectual property, they undermine the foundations of a vibrant culture and democracy."

Second, a writer who relies on AI to write for them can no longer legitimately claim authorship. To say otherwise is dishonest and fraudulent. As my publisher says, "Authors who want their names on a book cover must *write the book*."

Many publishers are also concerned about what might happen to our culture if "everyone is consuming chatbot regurgitations emitted by a few powerful companies." My publisher cites the following observations from neuroscientist Erik Hoel.

We find ourselves in the midst of a vast developmental experiment. [The culture is] becoming so inundated with AI creations that when future AIs are trained, the previous AI output will leak into the training set, leading to a future of copies of copies of copies, as content becomes ever more stereotyped and predictable. . . . Once again, we find ourselves enacting a tragedy of the commons: short-term economic self-interest encourages using cheap AI content. . . . which in turn pollutes our culture and even weakens our grasp on reality (*The New York Times,* March 29, 2024).

Even the overuse of an AI-based writing assistant could distract you from finding your own insights about your subject. The best scripts require the writer to become deeply familiar with how the character speaks and behaves in each situation. The character might stumble over words in a romantic setting, or perhaps use powerful words as a weapon when threatened, or repeat phrases as a means of pushing her agenda on others. Only you, after extensive research, can capture these nuances. An algorithm will merely regurgitate information from thousands of sources. It cannot comprehend what you as a dramatist know about the art of drama. Only you can allow the character's story to interact soulfully with your own life experiences. The writing process will come to you through your intuition, emotions, and intelligence.

Writers must make up their own minds about how to use AI, but we need to remember that a script is not just text; it is a manifestation of an artist's unique creative vision—something AI cannot produce. I believe that audiences will never want generic films and plays; they will always desire what you and only you can create, not data reconfigured by a robot. Writing a powerful biographical drama requires you to define what *you* want to say—

at the deepest level—about your subject's life. Your message isn't something external to you; it is an expression of *who you are*.

As I stated earlier, be sure to seek professional legal counsel if you think your script could expose you to legal risks. Hopefully, this chapter will help you steer clear of getting into hot water so that you can relax and write your drama!

CHAPTER 5

Is Your Subject Suitable?

On seeing Pam Gems's biographical drama about the painter Stanley Spencer, the celebrated British prose biographer Victoria Glendinning realized that the genre of biography was, in comparison to biographical dramas, quite limiting.

"How much more exciting to throw away the documentation and write a play," she said. "And how much more difficult and dangerous" (Coveny, 2011).

Danger and excitement derive from dramatic license, which is granted to bio-dramatists but forbidden to nonfiction biographers. In fact, prose biographer Ken People, author of *Stanley Spencer: A Biography* (1991), was upset by Gems's cavalier approach to documentation. In a terse letter to The National Theatre, which staged Gems's biographical drama, People wrote, ". . . this material has been rearranged—distorted to the purist—in the interests of stagecraft" (Rosenthal, 2018). People may have disliked the biographical drama about Spencer, but audiences and critics felt differently. The play had a sold-out season and won Play of the Year at the Oliviers.

Clearly bio-dramatists have more freedom to arrange facts in ways that increase drama, add excitement, and provide deeper insight. But with that freedom comes tremendous difficulty and risk. Purists might respond with disdain!

Another cause for contention is that biographical dramas often portray what is ultimately unknowable. The full truth about a person will always be unattainable. Mystery will always abound, which can lead to unending disputes. As Peter Arnott succinctly explains: "I can't know. I wasn't there."

Nevertheless, audiences are keen to see life stories onstage or onscreen, and those stories are usually written by people who did not see the actual events. And audiences want to see these stories presented in beautiful, powerful, meaningful, and dramatic forms—as they should. So, the bio-dramatist might enjoy the freedom offered by artistic license, but he or she must also embrace and accept responsibility for the dangers and difficulties.

Accepting that responsibility is essential as writers evaluate whether an individual would make a good subject for a biographical drama. A writer might be enthralled with a person's life, but if the writer cannot see a way to shape a high-quality biographical drama based on that subject, then exuberance might be in vain.

To evaluate the dramatic suitability of a subject, writers need to think about some basic criteria. This chapter is designed to help you consider those criteria as you assess the suitability of your subject—before you start to write.

Is the Subject's Life Dramatic?

Not all life stories make good drama. So, the first question you should ask is: What makes your subject's life powerfully dramatic?

Drama can be defined as "a written composition involving conflicts and emotions through action and dialogue designed for a performance." Does your subject's life meet the definition of drama?

I have a friend who has had an interesting life. He is from a lower-middle-class family in a suburban Australian city. Early on, he had no connections within the film or theater industry. Nevertheless, he became a hugely successful screenwriter and Hollywood champion. This sounds like a dramatic life! However, on closer examination, his life did not exude dramatic emotion; rather, his life was filled with years of hard work until he became excellent at his craft. He was an even-tempered and calm person. No addictions, no steamy affairs with famous stars, no nasty divorces, no criminal activity, no theft of his great ideas, no exciting obstacles to overcome. He had a stable social life, which fed his success. Thus, he was a less-than-ideal subject for a biographical drama.

Let's face it: People don't want to sit for a couple of hours to watch a biographical drama unless the subject's life is dramatic. If it is a story about a subject's extraordinary achievements, audiences want to see the sacrifices that success required. Drama needs to include, among other things, human vulnerability. Scenes of a writer spending hours and hours at a desk honing his craft are not that interesting.

By contrast, when I was asked to write *Barassi*, I saw a dramatic shape to his life that immediately excited me. His life was full of highs and lows. His ambition led to success, but also to great hardship. I wanted to reveal his obsession to be the best and to win. I also wanted to understand how he coped when he stopped getting what he so desperately wanted.

The story of whistleblower Katharine Gun, who had absolutely everything to lose and nothing to gain when she leaked an official secret memo, led bio-dramatist and director Gavin Hood to write her story. Gun leaked a document to hold governments to account, to stop a war, and to save lives. Hood's biographical drama *Official Secrets* (2019) follows her tumultuous journey, including the devastation she experienced when her act of courage failed to stop the war and nearly landed her in prison.

My point is this: An amicable person with a lot of good luck might make a solid friend or suitable partner, but unless the subject's life is full of mystery, hardship, and obstacles, he or she will probably make a boring character. I'm not suggesting that biographical dramas need to be about someone famous, but the person's story must contain dramatic elements.

Hollywood scriptwriter and director Joseph Mankiewicz identified one of the main problems facing bio-dramatists. "The difference between life and the movies is that a script has to make sense, and life doesn't" (Lower and Palmer, 2001). Real life is often undramatic, long, and meandering. Most people amble through their objectives, jobs, relationships. Most of us don't have intriguing, heart-stopping antagonists. By contrast, film and play characters must face compelling obstacles. All good stories must be plausible yet dramatically engaging. For a real story to be turned into a performed story, the subject's life must be conducive to shaping a compelling narrative. You must be able to see something in your subject's life that excites and intrigues you, and that can also be presented in dramatic form. In most cases, this will mean fudging some facts.

Your Subject's Life and Dramatic License

We have already discussed the ethical issues surrounding dramatic license. Here I want to write about the use of dramatic license as it pertains to choosing or rejecting a biographical drama subject. You might have a person in mind whose life story has the potential to make a great biographical drama—if you have freedom to embellish the facts. But how much artistic freedom would that require?

Playwright and screenwriter David Mamet said, "In dramatic biography, writers and directors end up reverting to fiction. To be effective, the dramatic elements must and finally will take precedence over any 'real' biographical facts" (Mamet, 1998).

Audiences usually don't demand bio-dramatists to present perfectly accurate plays and films. They have already conceded that the actor is only a representation of the real person, and they know they are watching an artistic performance. They accept ambiguity and want to experience great drama.

That said, dramatic license must, paradoxically, "ring true." Writers must offer a *dramatic* truth. Bio-dramatists must foster the audience's willing suspension of disbelief, meaning that the play or film must be plausible and honest. So, our job as writers is to help audiences accept our plays and films. The liberties we take with biographical dramas must be earned. We will look further at how to earn creative license later in the book.

Bio-dramatists have more freedom than prose biographers but less freedom than fiction writers. Biographical dramas require us to include facts and details that anchor the dramatic work to the real world. This anchor is a gift. It provides us with ready-made characters, a full social and historical context, a wealth of events, forms of speech, and potential narrative arcs. And yet, the bio-dramatist's freedom is limited. Audiences will challenge the truth of biographical dramas.

Ursula Canton surveyed audience members after seeing Nicholas Wright's play *Vincent in Brixton* (2003). The play dramatized Dutch painter Vincent van Gogh when he lived in a working-class suburb of London. Canton found that some survey participants were anxious about the veracity of theatrical performances. Many struggled to accept Wright's version of van Gogh's life because it was so different than the story they had encountered before. One survey participant said that accepting Wright's depiction of the painter's life could be regarded as "being stupid." Canton's research suggested that audiences will accept and even expect dramatic license, but they have limits. There is a crucial juncture at which an audience's trust might be lost (or earned). Audiences love the dramatic medium, but if a drama strays too far from factual plausibility, they usually lose interest or even get upset.

Motti Lerner seeks to balance historical facts with the subject's thoughts and emotions. "I think that I'm doing my best not to change the historical facts of the biography of the character, but I have full freedom to invent his or her internal journey." Lerner's point is important. Writers should uncover the factual history of a subject's activities and work, but the subject's emotional journey is more difficult to know and therefore it must be invented, at least to some degree.

David Hare's play *Stuff Happens* (2004) explores the reasons why US President George W. Bush and British Prime Minister Tony

Blair decided to invade Iraq. Hare uses direct quotes from those politicians' interviews and public appearances, but he invents what went on behind closed doors. In the author's note of the published play, Hare qualifies his use of imagination. "This is surely a play, not a documentary, and driven, I hope, by its themes as much as by its characters and story." Despite Hare's transparency about his creative license, *The Guardian's* Michael Billington described his experience viewing the play as follows: "One comes out enriched and better informed." Drama often evokes powerful feelings, which is one reason why people accept the dramatic version of the truth.

Bio-dramatists cannot know everything that happened, but we can utilize research, imagination, and dramatic presentation to make it *seem* like we were there. Writing dramatic truth is an effort to portray the *spirit* of the person's life and times.

In the film *At Eternity's Gate* (2018), screenwriters Julian Schnabel, Jean-Claude Carrière, and Louise Kugelberg show Vincent van Gogh recovering from a breakdown in a country hospital. In a confused state, he is lying in a bare, rickety hospital bed when his brother arrives from Paris. As his brother cradles him, we feel the profound love between the brothers and the extreme sacrifice they have made to enable van Gogh to make uncompromising art.

The scene is based on facts. Van Gogh was hospitalized. We know from surviving letters that his brother, Theo, did visit his brother. But the writer invented what they said and the action inside the scene. Despite some factual uncertainty, the emotional scene totally immersed viewers in that region of France in the 1880s. By the time the bedside scene occurs, the audience has already followed van Gogh's struggle, a journey that ended in his emotional breakdown. They have experienced van Gogh's authenticity as an artist and gained an intimate view of the challenges he faced. They have comprehended the sacrifices that dedicated artists and their families often make.

My point is this: Creative license is most effective when writers pursue the facts but strive to find the deeper, authentic thematic truth. This requires your subject's life to have the basic components of a powerful drama.

Another way to verify if your subject's life holds dramatic power is to search for the tensions between their deepest desires and the obstacles that stand against their ability to realize those dreams. Who or what opposes them? Van Gogh felt he must pursue his art even if it caused a mental breakdown. Bush and Blair believed they must invade Iraq even when the world was against it. Queen Elizabeth I had to maintain her power, even if it meant killing her cousin. Barassi wanted to win at all costs, but the cost meant he would lose everything else. Katharine Gun believed she must break the law to reveal the truth, even if it destroyed her life. Having a powerful antagonistic force in the subject's life will give a story power.

Will Your Audience Accept Your Subject?

When selecting a subject, you should think beyond your personal enthusiasm and consider whether the audience will find the person worthy of their time and money. In other words, you need to know your audience.

My producers for *Barassi* knew that many people in our audience would be football enthusiasts, especially older men who would bring family members to see the story about their football hero. My play about Edna Walling was performed at an Open Garden day in one of her famous gardens. So, I knew that my audience would comprise Edna Walling enthusiasts. I also knew that the audience for my work about John Lennon would include devout Lennon fans. I adapted each play to suit my audiences.

Try to discover your audience's preconceptions about your subject. British playwright and theater director Polly Teale discussed this question with me in relation to her play *Brontë*. She realized that her audiences would have clear preconceptions about the Brontë sisters due to their enduring fame. She understood that people watching the play might say, "This play is factually inaccurate," or "This is not what that sister would have done," or "This is not at all how I imagined her." When audiences are no longer willing to suspend disbelief, they fall away from the performance.

After conducting exhaustive research, Teale decided on a strategy to encourage her audience to accept her take on the Brontë sisters. In her words:

> You have to say, 'OK, this is my take on this story,' so now you make decisions. I mean the way I did it in *Brontë* really was by starting the whole piece in modern day and we watched them taking off their tracksuits, their trainers, and putting on the Victorian clothes and saying, 'Oh my god, can you believe they really wore this for tramping across the moors,' and you know, 'Oh my gosh, that's difficult to breath in.' So, we actually see them being constructed and we have the prop tables on stage. It was really clear that this was a construct. We weren't trying to say this is the slice of history, [or that] this is exactly what happened. We were saying, 'We're trying to imagine' (personal interview, 2016).

Her strategy, in other words, was to deliberately foreground the imaginative nature of her play as part of the play's action.

Willie Russell adopted a slightly different strategy in order to achieve the same effect. I asked him how he dealt with audience expectations in his 1974 musical about The Beatles, titled *John, Paul, George, Ringo . . . and Bert*. The play premiered at the Everyman Theatre in Liverpool, a city that, as Russell wryly remarks, was brimming with Beatles experts.

One of his solutions was to have a female folk singer perform the songs of the Beatles. This choice, he told me, "sidestepped invidious comparisons with the recorded version by the real thing." Russell also had the lead characters busk outside the theater, playing and singing Beatles songs in the street as audiences arrived. When these apparently opportunistic buskers surprised everyone by walking through the auditorium and getting on stage, the audience remembered that they were at a dramatic performance, not a documentary.

The Lehman Trilogy (2012) compelled audiences to accept a story that spanned 164 years right from the opening scene. The play starts in the modern boardroom of the financial company, which is famous for its collapse during the 2008 global financial crisis. The office is framed by glass walls and filled with sleek, modern furniture. We hear a 2008 radio news report about the firm's collapse. Due to the magic of theater, the company founder, Henry Lehman, a Bavarian immigrant in nineteenth century dress who had passed through Ellis Island in 1844, suddenly steps into the twenty-first century office.

Finding an Interesting Truth

The film *Yesterday* (2019) asks audiences to suspend plenty of disbelief. Richard Curtis's script asks people to believe an alternative universe in which The Beatles never existed and John Lennon is still alive. The film shows Lennon in his seventies and living happily with no knowledge that, in the alternative universe, he was a famous musician who was murdered at age forty. Yet he has the looks, glasses, and interests that the real Lennon had. This gives the scene poignancy and creates an interesting truth: Perhaps people are the same regardless of their life experiences.

In my research about Barassi, I learned that he travelled to his father's military grave in Libya and spoke to his dead dad for thirty minutes. This prompted me to write a scene in which the ghost of his father, at age twenty-six, talks to his forty-year-old son about his life. In other words, I portrayed a mixture of what really happened and my invented action. It was an "interesting truth" that was accepted and enjoyed by audiences. Positioning this scene early in the play also gave me confidence that I could write the entire work.

By contrast, controversy erupted over Michael Frayn's Tony Award-winning depiction of an afterlife meeting between physicists Niels Bohr and Werner Heisenberg in *Copenhagen* (1998). Frayn's work explores how we can never be certain of our thoughts, motivations, and memories. This theme made it clear to audience's that the play's objective was not historical, but philosophical. Nevertheless, Frayn's effort did not deter the critics. Historian Paul Lawrence Rose described Frayn as a Heisenberg apologist and accused him of "subtle revisionism . . . more destructive than [David] Irving's self-evidently ridiculous assertions—more destructive of the intensity of art, of science, and of history" (Paulin, 2002).

The Audience's Political, Philosophical, and Ethical Frameworks

Even if a bio-dramatist could perfectly represent the facts of a person's life, the audience might still reject the character—not because they doubt the truth presented in the play, but because they hold cultural, moral, or philosophical positions that make it hard for them to accept the subject.

Controversy is usually more prevalent in plays about blatantly evil characters. If a writer humanizes them, audiences might assume the biographical drama is apologizing for the subjects' destructive impacts. David Edgar's play about Hitler's architect, *Albert Speer* (2000), caused debate about whether Edgar's representation of the Nazi leader had served historical justice. In light of the immense suffering caused by Speer, some people criticized Edgar for humanizing him. In defense of his script, Edgar wrote the following in *The Observer*:

> As screenwriter Paul Schrader argued in defense of *Taxi Driver*, if writers stopped inventing criminals, 'we would still have psychopaths, but we wouldn't have art. We would still have Raskolnikovs, but we wouldn't have *Crime and Punishment*.' If Gitta Sereny hadn't written her book about Albert Speer, his slave workers would still have died, but we would be less able to understand why. For that reason alone, it seems to me worth taking the risk of putting his story on stage (Edgar, 2000).

A pertinent question driving many biographical dramas about

excoriated historical figures is: Why was the subject like that? I agree with Edgar that this question is worth examining. I would go further and ask: Why was she or he *allowed* to be that way? What social and political circumstances permitted such acts to happen? The answer to those questions might help us move toward a more just and humane society. However, if you choose to write a story about a controversial figure, be aware that you might ignite a firestorm!

Timidity is also detrimental. Oversensitivity to an audience's potential discomfort could reduce the quality of the script. For example, consider a biographical play by Jonathan Maitland about TV presenter Jimmy Savile titled *An Audience with Jimmy Savile* (2015). Savile was convicted post-mortem of sexually abusing hundreds of victims while the entertainment industry, media, police, and even the royal family ignored decades of rumors about him. Yet when I saw the production, I was left none the wiser as to why Savile had been able to commit so many crimes against children. I could not understand how a leering, angry, control freak (as performed by Alistair McGowan) could have fooled so many people.

The performance of *Savile* gave insight only into the subject's dark side. Maitland stuck closely to the facts of Savile's crimes and shied away from showing how a monster could hoodwink a nation. The result was a production that feels more like a police report than a drama. Perhaps Maitland did not want to show how Savile used charm and intelligence to deceive everyone, for fear of glamorizing him and thereby offending his victims. Ben Lawrence of the *Daily Telegraph* said, "The problem is that the play is all exposition, a detailed explanation of events (as far as we know them) that is completely lacking in drama" (Lawrence, 2015). The public loved the real Savile for decades. He was even knighted by the queen.

He must have had a charming public persona. Therefore, the play's understatement of his popularity shielded the audience from what could have been a much more powerful play, one that mirrored Greek tragedy by demonstrating how so many people became complicit to his crimes.

The Right Time to Portray Your Subject

As you evaluate the suitability of your subject, you should consider the context of your times in relation to the subject's history. In 2005, when a bio-dramatist touted the amazing story of whistleblower Katharine Gun, the writer found that producers did not want to go near an Iraq War story. It was too soon after the event and they believed audiences would be tired of the subject. The story wasn't filmed until 2019.

Working as a dramaturge at a London theater in 2000, I noticed that many good plays set in the Bosnian War were being passed over. Theaters thought that audiences would not be interested in events that had recently played out in the news. One of my early creative writing teachers said that it is best to wait at least ten years before writing about true events. Waiting promotes objectivity. Willie Russell agreed with this view, saying he needed time to process events before writing a play or a film.

Criticism of *The Social Network* focused on the fact that the events in the film were only six-years old. Critics said the writer could not fully portray the impact that Mark Zuckerberg and Facebook had made on the globe. By contrast, *The King's Speech*, written decades after the events, was able to show how King George faced his stuttering and effectively led his nation during World War II. It is a film that speaks to Britain's current confusion over national identity.

Prolific bio-dramatist Peter Morgan also operates with a ten-year rule. "If you have distance from the events, then your story can work as an analogy or parable, rather than its literal narrative," he said. "People can watch the *Frost/Nixon* interviews and make associations that aren't just about Richard Nixon and David Frost. Because time has passed, the film can have an additional resonance through metaphor." As bio-dramatists, we can use the past to understand the present.

Writing a historical biographical drama isn't really about the past. For you (while you write) and for audiences (while they are watching and reading), the past will come alive, as if it were the present. They say rules are made to be broken; so, by all means, write about recent events in someone's life—if you believe you can overcome the concerns I've raised.

Can You Offer a New Perspective?

Should you write about someone whose story has been told before? Well, why not? Iconic people such as Marilyn Monroe, Napoleon Bonaparte, Cleopatra, Shakespeare, Albert Einstein, and Catherine the Great are endlessly fascinating.

However, the fact that a famous person has already received abundant attention can make it difficult for bio-dramatists to write something new. Audience perceptions about that subject could be set in stone. When I think of Abraham Lincoln, I visualize Daniel

Day Lewis, the actor who portrayed Lincoln, not the US five-dollar bill! So, I encourage you to look carefully at what other writers have produced about your subject and be aware of the subject's cultural legacy.

As I thought about how to write a short narrative concert about John Lennon, I knew that busloads of plays and films had already been made about him. I didn't want to cover ground that had already been trod. I found an interesting, and less well-known time of his life, during which he had been a "house husband." This revelation allowed me to focus the audience's attention on a particularly happy time in Lennon's tumultuous life, a time made more poignant because he was tragically murdered while his second son was still a young boy.

William Shakespeare has been the central character in many plays and films, which proves that one person's life can inspire many different stories and thematic directions. Edward Bond based his play *Bingo* (1973) on public facts known about Shakespeare's non-theater business dealings in Stratford-upon-Avon. Bond used Shakespeare's actions to create a metaphor designed to explore the role of writer/artist in a capitalist society. Bill Cain, who wrote the play *Equivocation* (2014), showed a noble Shakespeare resisting the manipulations of those in power when King James commissioned him to write a propaganda play about the Gunpowder Plot of 1605. There's an even more flattering treatment of Shakespeare in Lee Hall's popular play based on the film *Shakespeare in Love* (1998). Ben Elton speculated about Shakespeare's retirement years in Stratford-upon-Avon in his film cheekily called *All Is True* (2019).

Using one life story, these writers have created four different narratives and character perspectives. Bond asked audiences to reassess Shakespeare myths and to question other humanist writers who might not live by the values they espouse in writing. Cain explored the theme of courageously speaking truth in difficult times. Hall wrote about the love story that inspired Shakespeare to pen *Twelfth Night* (1602). And Elton speculated about the great man in retirement, and how an influential man might return to the simplicity he had fled as a young, ambitious man.

Modern audiences are primed to accept invention and several competing, even contradictory, versions of the same life. This can all add up to what José Rivera calls, "another voice in a larger conversation" (personal interview, 2016). Nevertheless, modern audiences are savvy! Most people have seen many biographical dramas. So, if you are planning to write about a person who has already received abundant attention in plays and films, you should find a way to add something new and important to the conversation.

Researching what other writers have produced about your subject will enable you to see your work in historical context. As writers, we should know whose shoulders we are standing on. Studying what other writers have done can open us to new ideas and exciting choices, emboldening us to be more daring.

Can You Portray Your Subject in Unconventional Ways?

Some potential biographical drama subjects have compelling lives and personalities, but they might lack unique qualities that engage hearts and minds. If that is the case with your subject, don't immediately give up. You might see a way to truthfully present the person's life in an *avant-garde* form. The artistry you bring to the script can transform a non-dramatic story into a vibrant work of art.

Two examples of *avant-garde* biographical dramas are Caryl Churchill's play *Top Girls* (1980) and Charlie Kaufman's film *Being John Malkovich* (1999). Churchill's play is set at a dinner party during which a woman from literature, history, and legend come together to enjoy a meal. *Being John Malkovich* involves fictional characters who somehow find a portal that leads into the mind of actor John Malkovich. The title character performs himself!

Howard Brenton was a game-changing biographical drama writer during the 1970s and 1980s. He was joined by Tom Stoppard, who wrote *Travesties* (1974), Caryl Churchill (mentioned above), and Howard Barker, who wrote *Victory* (1983). These playwrights blended fact with fiction, defied chronological order, and used non-realistic styles in their works.

As previously mentioned, Churchill made the bold choice to stage a dinner party during which famous women from ancient and recent history speak freely about their lives. Stoppard had no evidence that James Joyce, Tristan Tzara, or Vladimir Lenin had ever met when they all lived in Switzerland during the World War II, but he wrote a play in which all three men interact. Brenton's *Christie in Love* (1970) and *The Churchill Play* (1974) feature deceased historical figures who rose from their graves in a manner that parodied the horror genre. By dramatizing a resurrection that obviously never happened, Brenton demonstrated that a performed biography resurrects a character. By making the resurrection literal, Brenton revealed what it means for a writer to bring the dead to life on a stage.

In 2002, Kaufman again defied convention by producing his award-winning screenplay *Adaptation*, which is about a screenwriter struggling to write a biographical drama about orchard thief John Larache. The film focuses on a screenwriter who goes crazy while attempting to write a biographical drama.

Another example of an unconventional film is by Francois Giraus and Don Mckeller titled *32 Short Films about Glenn Gould* (1993). It portrays the Canadian pianist (Gould) in a way that eschews a traditional cause-and-effect narrative. The scenes comprise single clips, longer dramatic scenes, meditative animations, x-rays of a body playing the piano, and the pills the pianist consumed each day. The scenes give shape to the fragmented, contradictory life of a brilliant artist.

Sid and Nancy (1986) is a beautifully constructed screenplay about the (at times) tender relationship between two punks in 1970s Britain. The film portrays their lives beyond the piercings, chains, torn tee-shirts, and combat boots to reveal the vulnerable skin of an ambitious young woman who is keen to help her naive boyfriend get more out of his singing career.

I Shot Andy Warhol (1996) follows the life of a performance artist, starting with her painful childhood, then revealing her as a hard-working, struggling artist, and then showing when she shot Warhol. The script reveals that strange behavior can be a strategy to obtain what all of us long for—love and recognition.

The Passion of Joan of Arc (1928), by director and screenwriter Carl Theodor Dreyer, is based on the transcripts of Joan of Arc's trial. The transcripts told the story of how a country maid from Orleans, dressed as a boy, led French troops to defeat British occupation forces. After the trial, Joan was burned at the stake in 1431. Dreyer combined the transcripts into one imagined inquisition during which the judges try and fail to change her testimony. They can't overcome her courage and conviction.

The film *I'm Not There* (2009) boldly employs six actors to depict different facets of singer Bob Dylan's public personas. Screenwriters Todd Haynes and Oren Moverman weave in Dylan's songs with quotations, images, ideas, and album covers. By design, the film shows that Dylan's true essence remains elusive and, by extension, that the truth about any person is complex.

Summary

As you consider whether your subject is suitable for a biographical drama, it's helpful to ask the following questions: Is the person's life dramatic? If not, can you invent a framework that would elevate the drama while being careful with the facts?

Remember to be aware of your audience as you shape your story. Consider the ten-year rule when choosing a subject. If you hope to write about someone famous—in particular a person whose story has been presented before on stage or screen, discern whether you can add a new perspective that has never been presented before.

Writing Exercises

1) Go somewhere where you will not be interrupted. Write for around five minutes on each question shown below.

    a. What is it about the person you hope to portray that makes his or her story dramatic?

b. What is it about this person's story that makes it worthwhile to tell?

c. How might audiences respond to your character?

d. What forces of antagonism (inner and external struggles) were present in your subject's life?

e. Is this the right time to write your story? Are audiences ready?

f. Should you focus on just one period of the subject's life? If so, write about the dramatic elements of that period. Comb through the events of your subject's life and focus on one that is dramatic. Was this a time when your subject pursued a goal, overcame obstacles, or experienced hard-won success?

g. Can you portray your subject by writing an unconventional, *avant-garde* biographical drama?

CHAPTER 6

Research

The research process for writing a biographical drama is unique in relation to other forms of artistic writing. The bio-dramatist's goal is not to discover only historical facts; rather, the writer seeks to gain a deep understanding of *a person*. A biographical drama script shows not only what happened to the subject, but also the person's behavior, emotional struggles, family history, traumas, motivations, psychological wiring, emotional trigger points, physical condition, and relationships.

All research starts with good questions. However, people are so complex and mysterious that the questions a bio-dramatist might ask are virtually limitless. We can't ever know another person completely. This means that bio-dramatists, despite strong research efforts, will deal with conjecture, possibilities, unverified data, and many unknowns. In the pursuit of truth and accuracy, there will be gaps that only imagination can fill.

The types of questions writers ask will determine the direction of the research and, eventually, the outcome of the script. For bio-dramatists, the questions need to point toward a richer and deeper understanding of the subjects, while also searching for a dramatic narrative. From the perspective of good drama, what elements of the subject's life are most important? What events shaped that person? How did the subject behave in extreme circumstances? What gives his or her life order and meaning? How does the person relate with other people?

These types questions often emerge from the writer's own inner life. Commenting on the research process, screenwriting professor and playwright Sam Smiley advised dramatists to ask *themselves* the same questions that they ask about their subjects: "What is important in life? What gives life order and meaning? How do you behave in extreme circumstances? Where do human struggles lead?" (Smiley, 2005). He believes that writers need to become conscious of their own perceptions of the world, in part because deeper self-understanding will help them research and comprehend the inner depths of the people about whom they write.

While researching for my play *Barassi,* I wanted to solve the mystery of how a person who had a difficult childhood and no natural athletic ability as a child could become a top Australian football player and coach. That I was so fascinated by that aspect of Barassi's life revealed a lot about me, the questioner. My curiosity extended from my own anxieties about becoming successful at something, and from my self-doubts. Rivera asked, "What am I if I lived this person's life?" But I approached my play from a different angle: *How might Barassi be like me?*

This connection between the writer's research questions and the writer's deepest sensitivities and life experiences can empower the writing process. As understanding of our subject grows, and as we find a strong connection with the subject, we can write the biographical drama with more authority and passion.

Biographical dramas, however, require writers to move beyond their own experiences and feelings. We must also look outside of ourselves to confront and explore what we don't understand about our subjects. That is the nature of curiosity. Sincere curiosity about a person leads to fascinating discoveries, which in turn opens the door to more creativity. *How might Barassi be like me?* is a good starting question. But Rivera's question, "What am I if I lived this person's life?" requires a greater feat of imagination, which is essential to biographical narratives.

Thinking outside yourself compels you to dig deeper. Imagine that you're writing about a person whose occupation is foreign to you. If you're locked within yourself, you might ignore the professional aspects of your subject's life, whereas strong curiosity would lead you to spend extended time in your subject's workplace. If your biographical drama will be set in a long-past era, curiosity will motivate you to learn all that you can about the social and political milieu that shaped your subject. If your subject was shy and you are outgoing, then thinking outside yourself will help you discover what it is like to be shy in an extrovert's world.

As discussed earlier, bio-dramatists enjoy some freedom to dramatically portray facts. There are many kinds of scripts; therefore, there is no one-size-fits-all template for researching a biographical drama. To a large extent, the research process will be shaped by your artistic vision and ambition, and by your subject. But all research deals with two categories: 1) *what* to look for, and 2) *how* to look for it. The rest of this chapter explores those two categories.

What to Look For

This book's first chapter provided insights into the power and nature of biographical dramas. I encourage you to integrate the lessons from that chapter into the research phase of writing your script.

What should you look for as you conduct research?

Discover Your Subject's Social Context

The society in which we are raised shapes us—sometimes throwing us badly out of shape! For that reason, a critical aspect of biographical drama research is to study the social milieu in which your subject lived. Discover how the person's social situation affected his or her behavior, values, and beliefs. Did the person rebel or acquiesce to that society?

One of my characters, Edna Walling, was a lesbian who operated her own landscaping business in Australia of the 1920s and built her own suburb. To better understand Walling, I had to investigate the social barriers she had to overcome as a gay woman in that era. A similar process of learning took place while I wrote *Barassi.* He grew up in a time—the 1950s—that was foreign to me, so I had to spend many hours researching the society that shaped him.

I discovered that, in the 1950s, the deaths, physical injuries, and psychological traumas endured by Australia's World War II soldiers still cast a long, dark shadow. As I watched interviews with soldiers and their families, I came to better understand an era during which the idea of glory in sacrifice was strong. I learned that the authority of church and state was rarely questioned, and that people glorified masculine values, such as *mateship,* a colloquial Australian term for a deep friendship, mainly between two males. This cultural value impacted how Australians saw themselves. My research revealed that comradery between men at war, where interdependence was a life-and-death issue, was transferred post-war to the football field.

Melbourne citizens in the 1950s were obsessed with football. In the pre-television era, football dominated the public's entertainment options. Because I hadn't lived through that period, I struggled to understand why the sport held such a strong grip on people. I talked to my parents and others who lived in Melbourne during that time. My parents and many of their friends had migrated to Australia with no knowledge of Australian football. Yet many of them found an entrée into an active social network as soon as they chose a football team to support. When people pledged allegiance to a club, usually located near home, they spent each Saturday with other migrants who shared a common passion. Football enabled Australians to form friendships. Football eased the loneliness of migrants.

Learning about that period in Australian history developed my imagination. Research showed me why my character became such an important part of local history.

If possible, I recommend that you visit the town and house of your subject's childhood. Walk where he or she walked. Actor David Morrisey, who won a BAFTA award for his portrayal of British Prime Minister Gordon Brown, made a trip to Brown's childhood town. Morrisey says: "Whilst the people are friendly, the environment is dull, dark, and it's often throwing it down with rain. It's a harsh place and there can be a cutting wind. You've got to be tough to survive that environment and the sheer battle against the elements gives you ideas about posture" (Cantrell and Luckhurst, 2010). He added that Brown had an accident in his teens that nearly blinded him. Morrisey believes that accident explains why Brown lived in a constant hurry.

The script for the film about painter Vincent van Gogh, *At Eternity's Gate*, by Jean-Claude Carriere and Julian Schnabel, revealed van Gogh's intensely spiritual relationship with nature. It was filmed in Arles, where van Gogh spent his final years and produced many of his masterpieces. The film feels especially poignant when you realize that the paths the actor walked are the same paths that van Gogh walked more than a century earlier. All those textures in the film are the result of the writer's immersive research.

You may not be able to afford overseas travel, but there is Google Earth! Or you could try a verisimilitude. Imagine that your subject is Shakespeare. You learn through research that he walked and, when he was more prosperous, rode a horse to London from Stratford on Avon. Unfortunately, you live in Adelaide or Vancouver. No worries: Try walking the same distance Shakespeare walked in a similar region near you. Even better, ride a horse!

You want your script to have its roots in facts, but the script's trunk, branches, and leaves should blow freely in the wind of invention. Immersing yourself in the physical location of your subject's life—childhood neighborhood, university, workplace, etc.—will help you root the script in fascinating facts. Try to find *specific* details about your character's life. Perhaps he or she loved gardens, books, houses, or paintings. If your subject was a priest, doctor, soldier, or nurse, consider spending a day or more in that person's uniform and observe how people treat you. (Don't get into any trouble with this advice, please!) If your character lived in the distant past, wear clothes from that period. I dressed in Edna Walling clothing, including jodhpurs and gum boots, and I walked through as many of her gardens as I could.

If your character is from another century, imagine a candlelit room at night. Does your subject walk through a world without phones or electricity, or does the person live in a big, noisy city in a tiny room, or in a grand manor house? What air did your subject breathe and what sounds did she or he hear? Consider the smells and sights. What effect did all of that have on the subject? What was the fabric of the person's clothing like? The more you can place yourself deep inside your subject's world, the better you will be able to reproduce your character with intimacy.

Search for the Subject's Inner Motivations

I discovered that Barassi's primary motivation was to live up to his war-hero father. Once I found that, I moved closer to finding the engine of my play. If you can unlock what motivates the lead character, you will clarify your biographical drama's theme, story structure, character, and tone. The person's inner motivation links biography, character creation, and dramatic craft.

Sometimes the subject's external life exists in contradiction with his or her inner world. If so, that makes for great drama! Polly Teale, in her research about the Brontë sisters, found that from a young age they wanted to be writers. Yet, when they were growing up, the local Yorkshire library in Haworth only allowed men and boys to be members. In those days, women were not expected to read and certainly not to write. This type of gender segregation shaped the sisters' *outer* world into a conservative and restricted veneer. Meanwhile, their *inner* world erupted from the books, letters, and journals they wrote—and it was wild, vivid, and passionate.

Teale's research included going to Haworth in Yorkshire to experience the outer world of the sisters. She explored the muddy moors, the austere landscape, and the hard sofa on which Emily died. This knowledge helped Teale write her play in a way that revealed both the inner and outer worlds of the sisters.

Discovering the Person in Details

While researching your subject, jot down seemingly small but interesting facts that, in a script, might reveal more about them. For instance, was your character tidy or messy? What did the person's house or apartment look like? Did it contain books, art works, or modern furniture? What about the subject's personal grooming habits? Was he or she obsessed with appearance? Was the person's hair greasy, stylish, or neat? What about the state of the subject's car, bicycle, horse, or shoes? Tom Stoppard found out that one of his characters, A. E. Housman, bequeathed a pair of shoes to his manservant. These small details serve as powerful clues about the character's true nature and personality.

Study the Subject's Speech

A major difference between a prose biographer and a bio-dramatist is that the latter, in the main, invents the subject's dialogue. In most cases, biographical drama writers have not witnessed firsthand the subject's actual conversations. The real person, unless verbatim speech is used, never said most of the things that will be in the drama. However, the writer can find ways to study the tone, style, and manner with which the subject spoke.

Willie Russell was careful to research the way each member of The Beatles spoke before he invented the dialogue for *John, Paul, George, Ringo and . . . Bert* (1974). I listened to all of Barassi's available recorded speeches before I wrote the play's dialogue. Robert

Reid listened to many recorded shows that featured late comedian Bill Hicks. This enabled him to capture the subject's cadence and confidently invent the dialogue for his play *Screaming in America: The Bill Hicks Project* (2002). Reid captured his speech so well that those who managed Hicks's estate thought that Reid had used the comedian's copyrighted work (personal interview, 2016).

If no audio source material is available, consider how your subject's accent, cadence, and vocal tone might be developed. You can glean a lot about speech from the person's life, social context, and education.

Humans often talk differently in private and public settings. Based on what you know about the subject's personality, consider how the person's speech might have sounded in intimate contexts and in public. For example, while researching for my play *Requiem for the Twentieth Century*, one of the characters was the much-loved Spanish playwright Federico Lorca. I found no record of how he spoke; however, I found and read a translation of his letters, as well as copies of his plays and poems. Based on those readings, I concluded that his speech was probably passionate and full of irony when he spoke in large groups, but soft and melancholy when alone with his lover.

Handling Uncomfortable or Complex Discoveries

There are dark and light shades to everyone. Your research is, therefore, bound to uncover facts that you might instinctively want to hide—or bring to light, depending on the nature of your subject. It's difficult to discover ugly sides to people we admire, and we usually like to reveal dirt about people we disdain.

While researching for my play about Edna Walling, I learned that she was a lesbian who never declared her sexuality. She lived in a time that was hostile toward gay women. Letters published in a prose biography revealed that she was in love with a woman, but they could never be together.

This discovery made me sad, but it helped me understand her volatility and incessant work habits. I faced a dilemma. On the one hand, I was uncomfortable about "outing" her when she had never outed herself. On the other hand, I was also uncomfortable with excluding her sexuality. She was a successful, intensely talented, gay woman who should be celebrated! In the end, I left her sexuality out of the play. I decided to concentrate on her passion and her fight to create her greatest garden.

While writing *Barassi*, my research also uncovered difficult information about him. I found many incidents in which Barassi used bullying tactics and violence to control his players, which was not unusual for the time. The more I learned, the more complex my emotional reaction became. For example, his bullying alarmed me even though his motivational speeches and determined focus earned my respect. I greatly admired Barassi when I was a child, but now I had to negotiate that admiration with my growing knowledge of his less admirable traits.

The point is this: A negative reaction to an aspect of the subject's life can be useful as an early indicator of both the writer's bias and how an audience might react. Keep that in mind if you discover uncomfortable character traits about your subject.

This discussion about what to look for in research is not exhaustive. Research should be approached as an adventure, an exploration into unknown territory. Always be prepared to learn something new. You never know what you might find.

How to Conduct Research

This section is not designed to be a college class in research methods. Rather, I hope to give you a general framework for how to approach research and share a few ideas that I've found helpful. I'll also share ideas from the renowned writers I have interviewed.

Stages of Research: Wide to Narrow, General to Specific

Research generally begins with a broad view of the person's life. In the initial phases, you should learn as much as you can about your subject's life until decisions are made about what specific elements of his or her story to focus on. Then you can begin to narrow your research.

For example, I read widely about Federico Lorca's life. I learned a great deal about his personality from the letters, poems, and plays he had written. I discovered that many of his friends had implored him to flee to Mexico when Spain's civil war was breaking out.

I then narrowed my focus and wrote a scene set in a bar, the Casa Labra in Madrid, that Lorca frequented just prior to the outbreak of the war. In the scene, Lorca argues with his artist friends who plead with him to leave for Mexico. He decides to remain in Spain and travel back to his home in Granada.

Then my detective work became more specific. I researched about Madrid in 1936. I read about Casa Labra and searched online to see photos of its interior. (If I had had the money, I would have loved to have gone there.) I studied the other artists he knew in Madrid. As a result, my focus shifted to those artists, including Pablo Picasso and Salvador Dali, whom I included in the scene. I studied the small details of that place and time, including the drinks that people would have consumed at the bar. So, even though I invented the artists' meeting at Casa Labra, I authentically portrayed other details.

When I found an article about Lorca's last amorous relationship, I knew that Lorca's real reason for staying in Spain— even though his life was in danger—was love. Lorca told everyone that he was remaining in Spain to complete his sonnets of dark love. In reality, he didn't want to go to Mexico without his lover.

As another example of how research moves from the general to the specific, consider the work of José Rivera's biographical drama about Che Guevara's early life, titled *The Motorcycle Diaries*. Rivera first widened his research to encompass Che's whole life. Then he focused on the specific events of when Guevara went on a road trip through South America in 1952. During the general research phase, Rivera learned that Guevara, while imprisoned in a remote Bolivian school just before his execution in 1967, formed a new friendship with a schoolteacher. This story fascinated him, but it wasn't directly relevant to the screenplay. So, Rivera went back to his research a few years later to write the play titled *School for the Americas,* which concentrated on the last two days of Che Guevara's life.

Research that you don't use now could become another biographical drama!

Vox Populi

The Latin term *vox populi* means "voice of the people." As a research method for biographical drama writers, *vox populi* provides a chance to hear directly from people who knew or know your subject. Those people can be an invaluable source for understanding your subject more intimately and lead you down surprising paths.

While working on *Barassi,* I conducted *vox populi* research by approaching strangers in the street. Using a digital recorder, I spoke to about one hundred people to learn what they knew and thought about Barassi. I could do that because Barassi was famous in Australia. My approach might not work for less famous subjects, but you can still use the *vox populi* method by speaking to people who knew (or know) your subject. Listen carefully and let people speak for as long as they want. You often get the best bits after you tell them the interview is over.

In his helpful book titled *Playwriting: The Structure of Action*, Sam Smiley says that writers "can beneficially tune in on the conversations of friends, family, and strangers. They can even note the types of issues they themselves discuss." The writer's goal is to discover the way people think and talk, the beliefs they hold, and how they express them. Ultimately, you want to recreate a believable, fully formed world, with authentic dialogue—a world that an audience will feel is true.

In the process of talking to strangers about Barassi, I learned that he provoked many different feelings in people. I learned about events in his life that people most remembered. I heard popular myths about him. I discovered small useful details, such as his way of saying, "If it is to be, it is up to me." I compiled a list of characteristics that people found most fascinating about him, which helped me decide which parts of his life to include in the play.

Research Your Subject's Contemporaries

A method that is related to the *vox populi* approach involves reading biographies and articles about people who were related to, worked with, or somehow knew your subject. For my work on *Barassi*, I read sports biographies from his era to see how others viewed him. You might be surprised by the views of your subject's peers. Perhaps your lead character was loved at work but loathed at home!

Sometimes disparate bits of research combine to trigger an idea. I found an interview with Barassi's second wife, Cherryl Copeland, in a book about the wives of influential men. Copeland said the following about her husband:

> He grew up with the hero notion of himself on the Saturday matinees and the war-hero father who died when he was three. He used to walk to school every morning along an avenue of honor of trees. So, he grew up with this hero notion of his father and himself. He pitted himself against everything all his life and I find that very heartening and endearing (Mitchell, 1994).

This information helped me write a scene in which I used a video as a stage backdrop. During the performance, audiences saw the young Barassi kick a football along a row of trees planted in his father's honor while the video projection showed the trees turning into soldiers. It turned out to be one of the audience's favorite scenes.

Bio-dramatist Anthony McCarten's research consisted of

"mainly talking to the band" when he wrote the screenplay about Freddie Mercury, the lead singer of Queen. As a result, much of the film presents the views of the surviving band (McDonald, 2017). In this film, which resembles the story of the prodigal son, Mercury fights with the band members and resigns from the group. According to the film, he went off the rails and had to beg the members to return. However, Mercury actually had a dazzling solo career while remaining an active Queen member. McCarten may have had to appease the remaining members of the band, who also happened to be producers of the film.

Sometimes people refuse to share what they know. The writers of the 2007 documentary titled *The Making of the King*, about Australian comedian Graeme Kennedy, revealed that many of Kennedy's friends and colleagues didn't want to talk. They sensed there was a conspiracy, that all of Kennedy's friends had been "got to." So, the writers needed to depend on other people who were disloyal to and critical of Kennedy. That probably led film critics and audiences to describe the subsequent film *The King* (2007) as dark and unflattering to Kennedy.

So, make sure to speak to a wide range of people. Seek a balanced perspective. Don't be idle in your research.

Researching the Supporting Characters

The better the script, the more likely you will attract the best actors, including those who will play the supporting characters in the biographical drama. As you research the story, you should study the other people in your subject's life, such as parents, spouses, children, serious friendships, lovers, and work colleagues.

Choose carefully the people you include in the script because audiences can only keep track of a few people. As you study the supporting characters, consider how each one shaped your subject's life. Were they antagonistic or supportive? What would your subject's life have been like if the supporting characters hadn't existed?

The Post-Research Phase

José Rivera warned that research can be the best form of procrastination. He was right. Research can become addictive—hard to quit. It allows us to put off the work of writing. So, when *should* we end the research phase?

I believe it's time to stop when we have reached what Rivera calls the "glutted" moment, that point when we feel we've done all that is needed. Immersive research can result in information overload. When you feel overloaded, that's a good sign that you've reached the glutted moment. The point is not to acquire reams of facts, but to allow the facts to suggest a story and a shape for the biographical drama.

Once you've reached the glutted moment, you should take a step back and allow what you have learned to form a narrative shape. During this gestation period, you might benefit from writing a short outline.

Edward Albee endorses the idea of allowing the script to form in your mind before you begin writing the first draft. Although you will have ended your research, you will still be "discovering" and shaping your character for the audience. Trust that you have completed the research and reassure yourself that you are an authority on the subject. This confidence will give power to your dramaturgical choices.

Allowing the facts to stew before making subjective writing choices is essential to the creative process. Neurologist Oliver Sacks discussed the importance of patiently allowing the brain to ingest source material before attempting to write a creative work. In the following rumination, which is worth quoting in full, Sacks contrasted Harold Pinter's creative process with that of an unnamed playwright, both of whom had adapted Sacks's memoir *Awakenings* (1973).

> In 1981, I got a letter from Pinter in which he said that he had read *Awakenings* when it came out in 1973. He had immediately thought, *This is stuff for stage,* but he couldn't think how to deal with it, and he put it out of his mind, and it had stayed out of his mind for seven years. But then, the previous summer, in the summer of 1980, he said he had a dream, didn't know what it was, but he awoke with the first words and the first scene of the play in his mind, 'Something is happening.' And the play then wrote itself in three days. So, this was a wonderful description of what I regard as almost a paradigm of the creative process, that first there is wrestling with a problem consciously and not getting anywhere. And then you let it go and you forget it. And then it has been incubated outside at levels inaccessible to you, so you don't know anything is happening, and when it's ready, it erupts into consciousness. What FWH Myers calls 'subliminal uprush.' These are the three stages Poincaré speaks about with mathematical invention, and I think these were the three stages, which Pinter has talked about, and he included the play, which I . . . read with great delight. The more so, as seven years earlier I had been sent a play also inspired by that particular case history

from a playwright in Philadelphia who said that he had just read *Awakenings* and he was so excited, he said he was obsessed by what was going on and . . . and he'd written this play, and it was . . . going to be shown in Philadelphia and would I like to come to the opening? And I wrote back and said, 'Slow down a bit, you know, this has not been discussed.' I said, 'In fact, there is already . . . a dramatic option has been taken on *Awakenings*, and I think . . . you need my permission. And . . . if I like it, we'll find a way of doing things.' He sent me the play and I cringed as I read it. I cringed because it was so close to *Awakenings*. I cringed because it was . . . a parroting and a paraphrasing and an aping and a mimicry of *Awakenings*, and I wrote back, I used some excuse, I said, 'I'm very sorry but, in fact, the patient herself and her large family are alive, you know, and this will definitely be seen, and . . . I don't think you can go ahead.' But I felt that this playwright, you know, had immediately regurgitated *Awakenings*, and he had not let it go down into the depths, and this . . . this struck me as, you know, the Pinter play brought home the difference between real creation . . . and this sort of mimicry (Sacks, 2011).

For added advice, I turned to Tom Stoppard during his 2011 talk at the Sydney Opera House. While discussing his biographical dramas *The Invention of Love* and *The Coast of Utopia*, he stated that he was less concerned about doing exhaustive research than he used to be.

You have to just cross your fingers, get into it and see where it takes things, where it takes you. And then, in some way, in ways I don't wish to begin to analyze, the play is doing some of the work for you. You can make all sorts of plans if you like, but if you . . . treat it like its own organism, with its own system of blood vessels, it'll actually take you places and then something that you were worrying about, suddenly the play provides the answer; 'My goodness what a stroke of luck.' Of course, it's not actually luck. It's your subconscious working for you all the time. I think you have to be the blind beneficiary of your subconscious. Allow it to fall off the end of your pen. Something I always trust; if it's any good at all, you have to lead it some of the time but follow it some of the time as well (Stoppard, 2011).

He emphasized that writers need to find a balance between following a predetermined structure and allowing the research to lead us. In other words, we should let lines "fall off your pen" and be humbly grateful when they are killer lines.

After research, writing requires imagination, and imagination takes time to develop. Michael Frayn, in his postscript to the 2010 edition of *Copenhagen*, wrote about the importance of imagination, saying: "But how far is it possible to know what [a subject's] train of thought was? . . . Even when all the external evidence has been mastered, the only way into the protagonists' heads is through the imagination. This indeed is the substance of the play" (Frayn, 2010).

So, the post-research phase should be used to allow your imagination to influence your work. Think of it this way: Biographical subjects function as a model for "imaginative extemporization." As discussed earlier, bio-dramatists cannot completely know their subjects. As a result, you will eventually begin to infuse your imagination into the work, interpreting the factual and historical elements through the lens of your mind and heart. That requires time, before you write, to let the research take shape.

Canadian bio-dramatist Sharon Pollack believes that "cutting and pasting" people's lives to "make a dramatic point" is her "unconscious intention" and is indeed the "most important thing you can achieve in a play" (Grace and Wasserman, 2006). Stoppard's "luck," Sacks's "ingestion," Frayn's "imagination," and Pollack's "unconscious intention" each refer to an ineffable and paradoxical process of writing a life story that has sprung from facts. There is a point where bio-dramatists must let what they have learned "go" in order to show up to the experience of writing; in other words, to allow their imaginations to "wright" the script into being.

So, soon, we shall begin writing.

Writing Exercises

1) Imagine you are having coffee with your subject. Write down four questions you would love to ask him or her. Chances are the audience will have the same questions. This could help organize your research as well as your script.

2) Is there a question about the subject that can be answered dramatically? In regard to the Brontë sisters, Polly Teale asked, "How is it possible that these three women who lived most of their lives out in the middle of nowhere on the Yorkshire moors, with so little life experience, wrote some of the most passionate, most erotic literature of all time?" Every scene of *Brontë* was pitched to answer that question. As Teale explained, "Answering the question acts as a magnet to draw certain things to the writing while other things will fall by the wayside" (personal interview, 2016).

3) To develop a writing style that grabs the reader, find the biographical drama scripts that you most admire. Published scripts can be found online or in libraries. Type your favorite script verbatim into a Word document. I did this with *Butch Cassidy and the Sundance Kid* (1969) by William Goldman and *Top Girls* (1982) by Caryl Churchill. You could transcribe at least a few of your favorite scenes. While you type the words, you'll gain surprising insights into the writer's mind and into why the script persuaded a film or theater company to produce it. I suggest you do this exercise with several scripts by different writers. Then write your own scene. It is always okay to stand on the shoulders of giants.

CHAPTER 7

Character Development

The allure of a biographical drama depends in part on the charm of the characters, the people who are vividly created in the script and then performed by actors. Many of the most successful biographical dramas are insightful character studies.

A strong character study requires the bio-dramatist to develop a deep connection with his or her subject. While writing *Barassi*, I realized that I had unearthed a connection between his inner personality and mine. Since then, I've learned that writers often become interested in characters who, at some profound level, are like them.

Barassi was one of the first television sports stars in Australia. I grew up watching him. So, it was a special moment when, as a young, suburban girl, I had the chance to see him in person. It was the mid-1970s and I was about eight or nine. I had attended a finals match during which my team, Richmond, was playing against North Melbourne, the team coached by Barassi.

In those days, the coach would give halftime advice to the players *on the field,* not in a locker room. Spectators sitting close enough could hear almost everything. On this mild winter's day, I witnessed Barassi storm angrily onto the field and give his North Melbourne players what is commonly described in Australia as a "spray." I had never been so close to a screaming man (who was not drunk). Barassi's voice, flamboyant dress, and fierce intensity made me feel an excitement I had never felt before. I saw that he cared deeply for his team and the sport. The advice he gave his players that day stayed with me.

Infusing his "spray" with passion, he demanded his players to stay in the moment, reminding them that a football game could change at any time. He told them to be ready to change with the game. Richmond was winning at halftime, but after Barassi's talk, North Melbourne went on to win the match.

As we caught the train home after the game, my brothers noticed how happy I was—even though my team had lost. They didn't know that I had been deeply inspired by the great motivator, Barassi.

Several decades later, I wondered if that speech had contributed to my decision to pursue a career in theater. In that intense world, every situation can be different and every show can change from one moment to the next. So, as I wrote *Barassi,* I realized what other bio-dramatists have discovered: a resonance between writer and subject. My early experience as a girl, when I watched Barassi on the field was, in a way, a theatrical one.

However, as a writer, I had to shed my simplistic, childish views of Barassi. As a coach, he would often use language such as, "You're playing like a girl" to humiliate his players. The language reflected a time in which accusing players of femininity was a severe sanction. Barassi's biographer, Peter Lalor, noted that Barassi once screamed at a young working-class man, commanding him to improve at football or "he would be nothing more than a shit plumber" (Lalor, 2010). On several occasions, Barassi shoved players violently into lockers and brick walls. Video footage shows that Barassi had a bad temper. I was drawn to Barassi for his better qualities, but I had to be careful not to present a revisionist view of his less palatable traits. I could not retroactively correct his non-progressive outlook, which he, along with the times, might have outgrown.

I also had to look at my own negative traits and come to terms with my volatile youth. I too had used bullying tactics on my mother and some of my friends to get what I wanted. I used those same traits to be successful in scriptwriting, which required a lot of determination, single-mindedness, and ambition. Some things I regret.

My experience is likely to be yours. You will probably find yourself developing an "imagined relationship" with your subject. Writing a biographical drama can feel like your subject is always on your shoulder, hopefully urging you on. Norwegian playwright, Henrik Ibsen, described his fictional stage characters not as actors in a drama, but as acquaintances. In the first draft, they were like strangers on a train. In the second, they were people he had known for a few weeks at a spa. By the last draft, "they [were] my intimate friends, they will not disappoint me, I shall always see them as I do now" (Edgar, 2009).

When writing about *a real person*, however, the journey to intimacy with that character takes place concurrently with research, conceptualization, and writing. This process feels less like inventing your subject and more like *absorbing* the subject. As Motti Lerner said, "I feel him in my heart. I feel him in my body." After months of work, you, like Ibsen, might eventually feel as though you intimately know your subject. The challenge for bio-dramatists, however, is to enable your audience to know the subject in an equally intimate way within a mere two or three hours.

This chapter focuses on how to portray and reveal aspects of your subject's deepest motivations, actions, and thoughts. Don't be surprised if you happen to see yourself in what you portray. If so, use that connection to your advantage. It will increase the power and authenticity of your script.

Characters and Dramatic Action

The true nature of a character is revealed by how he or she acts under pressure. There are three levels of dramatic action that your character may be exposed to: person against self, person against another character, and person against nature or society.

The first is *internal conflict*. The conflict might come from shyness, severe impatience, or an overly generous nature. Your subject might have an addiction. Perhaps your character is in a situation that results in cognitive dissonance. For example, Truman Capote in *Capote* (2005) was a successful writer who based his first nonfiction book on a killer with a similar upbringing. Capote had to fight feelings of love, empathy, and pity for a killer who had committed a horrific crime. And yet, to publish a bestseller, Capote had to write a strong ending, which required the execution of the killer.

The second is *external conflict*. In this case, your character might fight family members, lovers, or work colleagues. External conflict can emerge from those who try to prevent the subject from getting what she or he wanted. An example is Helen Keller's half-brother James in *The Miracle Worker* (1960). He adamantly asserts that there is no point to teaching Helen how to write, creating intense conflict with her and those who support her.

The third is *extra-personal conflict*. In this case, your character might fight sexism, racism, government departments, forces of nature, or institutions. Mahatma Gandhi in *Gandhi* freed his country from British rule. Erin, in *Erin Brokovich* (1983), successfully sued an energy corporation. Oskar Schindler in *Schindler's List* (2000) saved over a thousand Jews from the Nazi regime. Peter Arnott's central character in *White Rose* struggled against rampant sexism as she fought against Fascism. In *Ride Like a Girl* (2019), jockey Michelle Payne fought her father, industry sexism, and her health problems to become the first female jockey to win the Melbourne Cup.

As discussed earlier, a writer can't fully understand or portray everything about a person. People are too mysterious and complex, and research will never be complete. So, I next offer some ways to select the most dramatic aspects of your subject. Then I provide some ideas for how to *reveal* your subject's character in captivating ways.

What to Portray about a Subject

Let's first look at some vital aspects of a subject's character that work well in biographical dramas.

Compelling Motivations

In all forms of drama, characters are revealed by what they do (or did). Bio-dramatists gather facts about the subject's actions and then shape those deeds into a series of escalating dramatic scenes. Audiences want to slip into the character's skin and experience what he or she experienced. However, a bio-dramatist must also provide the audience with the *why* behind the subject's actions. The *why* can be subtle and it can be open to interpretation, but biographical dramas will only impact hearts and minds when the writer offers the most compelling, powerful reasons for the subject's choices.

That *why* should stir the audience to care deeply about the subject when he or she succeeds or fails. Bertie (King George VI) needed to overcome his stutter. Che Guevara needed to find his life's purpose. Mercury needed his band back. Salieri needed to take revenge on God. Joan, in *Red Joan* (2018) and *St. Joan* (1923), needed to be understood. Stan and Ollie needed to reconcile. Barassi needed to find peace with his father.

Your Subject's Inner and Outer Goals

The reasons that drive your subject's behavior are not simplistic. Humans are complex. People may have an outer goal—for example, to be the best at something—and have an inner goal of finding peace. Outer and inner goals can be at odds. An inner conflict can reveal something profound about a character and intensify drama.

In *Citizen Kane* (1941), William Randolph Hearst's external goal was to achieve great power and wealth. But, later in life, he longed for childhood innocence and simple happiness. Salieri set out to destroy Mozart as revenge against God, but he ended up destroying himself. In *The Motorcycle Diaries* (2004) the young Che Guevara's outer goal was to find youthful adventure, but the story reveals a restlessness rooted in a deeper need to find a life purpose.

Barassi was driven to win at football in order to please the ghost of his father, but the quest to be the best led to more misery than happiness. In *Judy* (2019*)*, singer Judy Garland needed to earn money to gain custody of her children, but the demands of work made it harder to care for her children.

A character's inner goal could be anything: to be accepted, to be safe, to be right. Often it takes a complete reversal of a character's outer goal to uncover the true, inner desires. These deep, hidden motivations will engage audiences.

A few years ago, I walked through the Biddy Mason Memorial park in Los Angeles. The park displays a series of plaques and art works that describe and honor the life of nineteenth century African American woman Biddy Mason. Mason was born a slave. After a hard fight petitioning for her freedom, she became a successful real estate developer and philanthropist. Biddy's life is a fascinating rag-to-riches story.

On the memorial plaques I read that she had been born into slavery on August 15, 1818 in Hancock County, Georgia. She had been sold multiple times, eventually landing at the Mississippi plantation of Robert and Rebecca Smith in 1836. After Robert joined the Church of Jesus Christ of Latter-Day Saints in the 1840s, he moved his family and fourteen slaves to many states, including California, even though it was illegal to have slaves there. (Smith hid them.) Mason walked behind the wagon.

After five years as a slave, Mason petitioned Judge Benjamin Hayes for freedom, who granted it. She then became a nurse and midwife, using the skills she had learned as a slave. Some patients gave her land in payment for delivering their children. She also saved her money and invested in downtown real estate on Spring Street, which would become her home. There Mason and others established the First AME Church, the oldest African American church in the city. Initial meetings were held in Mason's home. Among her many achievements, Mason opened an orphanage and a primary school for African American children.

We can reasonably assume that her life's outer goal was to be free and successful. But what about her inner goals? Perhaps Mason feared poverty, which could have driven her to do everything possible to achieve financial security. Perhaps her inner motivation was anger or revenge (success can be the best revenge). If so, that could have motivated her to upset the white-controlled system as the first African American to buy property in Los Angeles. What if her inner goal was to be accepted and respected by her peers?

My research about Mason has been far too superficial to make conclusions about these speculations, but my point is this: Your imagination as a writer, nourished by research, should help you decide what to portray about your subject's inner and outer goals. Remember that inner goals are most compelling when they conflict with outer goals. In a drama, we discover the most about characters when life puts them under pressure, when their primary goals are confronted by obstacles.

The Character's Fatal Flaw

Another way to add depth to a character is to reveal the person's fatal flaw. This device has been used by writers since the ancient Greeks. A "lack of self-awareness" is always a fascinating character flaw. Richard Nixon lacked self-awareness. "Overruling ambition" is another one. My character, Ron Barassi, had it. Shakespeare's

Richard III had it too. In *Angels in America,* Roy Cohn's flaw is his unquenchable thirst for power, as was Shakespeare's Macbeth.

However, try to avoid fatal flaws that are hard to understand and that stretch the audience's willingness to accept the story.

How to Reveal Your Character

Now that you have considered the complex nature of your character, you need to decide how to *reveal* that character to your audience.

Revealing Your Character through Images and Action

The writer transforms knowledge about a subject into images and action. A creative image or recurring visual can stimulate the audience's imagination.

In the 2019 film *Judy,* we see a young Judy Garland working on the set of *The Wizard of Oz* (1939). Then she plunges into a swimming pool as an act of rebellion, a moment in which she looks at us with a smile. It is a powerful image of a young woman who has a moment of happiness in her overly restrictive, demanding life. The consequences of her rebellion ricochet throughout her life.

While writing my play about Lorca, the Spanish dramatist, I had a recurring image of a man who would sit or stand behind people so that he could eavesdrop and write down what they were saying. He would shout "Terrible answer!" if he didn't like the way someone responded. This recurring image went from humorous to dangerous when he eavesdropped on two of the Spanish dictator

Franco's men.

A powerful image might also show a subject stalled in life. Prince Phillip, in *The Crown*, spends hours watching the 1969 moon landing on a Buckingham Palace television. As the astronauts land on the moon, the prince's inner turmoil about his lack of direction grows.

Mysterious characters can drive your writing. *The Assassination of Gianni Versace* (2018) includes an image of a young man in cheap white jeans and a tee-shirt standing outside the mansion where Versace lived. The audience sees only the back of the man, adding a sense of ominous mystery. We want to know what is going on in his mind, even though we suspect that he will soon kill Versace on the mansion's steps.

My research about Barassi revealed that his mother, Elza, rarely spoke of his dead father. She would only mention him when Barassi displeased her. She would say: "If your father was alive today, he'd be ashamed of you." This would deeply hurt the young boy (Lalor, 2010). Those scalding words from Barassi's mother enabled his father to hold a strong grip on his behavior—even though his father had died. The thought of a young boy trying to please his dead father moved me, so I created an image of the father as a hovering ghost.

Action is also a powerful way to reveal your subject's nature and behavior. What characters do, especially when under pressure, reveals a lot about them. Here are some examples of how writers have used action to portray the personalities of characters.

In my biographical drama about the children's writer Dr. Seuss, I wanted to display his eccentricity and playfulness, as demonstrated in his book *The Cat in the Hat*. I wrote: "Dr. Seuss is in a busy shoe shop. He walks to a display of women's shoes. He takes the sale prices from the display and places them on the expensive shoes. He goes about it as if he works there."

Actress Lana Clarkson was murdered by Beatle's record producer Phil Spector. Below is an invented scene based on Clarkson's alleged history of dating creeps. The actions in the scene I wrote show how easily Lana might have been duped by men.

> A man is waiting for his date to show up in a park. He has on a new shirt and it is itchy around the collar, so he has made his neck red with scratching. A beggar asks him for some loose change, and he ignores the beggar and checks his phone again while scratching his neck. A tall slim woman, Lana Clarkson, arrives with shiny blonde hair. She could be a model. He smiles at her eagerly, but she doesn't smile back and she tells him she hasn't got much time. He suggests they walk to the café nearby and they happen to walk past the beggar. The man gives the beggar a ten dollar note and Lana smiles at her date for the first time.

David Mamet's *Phil Spector* (2016) begins with the arrival of lawyer Linda Kenny Baden, played by actress Helen Mirren, who will take on Spector's case. Kenny Baden blows her nose. She explains that she was meant to be on an expensive holiday, so she needs a doctor and accommodations. It becomes clear in the first few minutes that she is ambitious because she chooses difficult work over health and holidays.

In *Trust* (2018), we first see oil billionaire John Paul Getty being dressed by his personal assistant while another man reads the coroner's report about the death of Getty's son. When his assistant says the word *suicide,* Getty groans in irritation. He seems more annoyed than distressed, but he soon focuses again on his clothes. We learn that he's more concerned about appearance than about his son's death.

What actions will reveal your characters? If you discovered in research that your character hated his job even though he was good at it, what action might reveal that trait? Barassi got many speeding fines and would talk over people and overbook himself for speaking tours. These facts inspired me to portray him rushing in and out of scenes while disregarding people around him and missing appointments.

Revealing Your Character through Dialogue

Playwright Suzan-Lori Parks believes that word *etymology* is a playwright's tool. She sees language as a physical act. "It's something which involves your entire body, not just your head. Words are spells which an actor consumes and digests, and through digesting creates a performance on stage" (Parks, 1995). She believes words give vital clues to actors.

Word choice and patterns of speech can reflect your subject's background, personality, age, status, and occupation. Dialogue is a wonderful way to reveal character and values. So, bio-dramatists need to be mindful that audiences are familiar with the ways that subjects speak. Audiences might *expect* to hear a unique syntax and mode of delivery from some subjects. So, if possible, find ways to incorporate their particular use of idioms and slang. I interviewed a former colleague of Barassi who often shared opinions by starting his sentences with, "In my book . . ."

Each line of dialogue should have a dramatic purpose and

create the illusion of being realistic, even though characters often speak more directly than people in real life. This can be a problem for bio-dramatists who use a subject's verbatim statements. Peter Cheeseman, who directed verbatim theater, affirmed that dialogue needs "an imaginative penetration of the source material" (Cheeseman, 1970). This "penetration" happens when writers select bits of dialogue and then subtract and add words that allow the language to impact the audience.

For example, my narrative tribute concert to John Lennon included dialogue spoken by the singer between songs. My job was to write a biographical story in short monologue form in the voice of Lennon.

While reading interviews with Lennon, I sensed that he wanted to "set the record straight." Knowing Lennon's inner motivations helped me energize the dialogue. The script became much more playable for the actor, or in this case, the singer.

Based on my casual interest in The Beatles, I knew that Lennon had been a househusband for several years. He raised his second son, Sean, from 1976 to his death in 1980. Lennon never had a father in his life and his uncle died when he was young, so he grew up as an only child with few male role models. He and his wife, Yoko Ono, had tried for ten years to have a baby, but they had many miscarriages and one stillbirth. So, when Sean was born, Lennon wanted to be a proper father. He admitted to feeling guilty about neglecting his first son, Julian. But during the years Lennon cared for Sean, people criticized him for wasting his musical talent.

A television interview with Beatle member Paul McCartney also stuck with me. McCartney affectionately remarked that Lennon didn't know how to play with kids. He said that Lennon, as a father, found it impossible to engage in the physical play and the make-believe games that kids like. He added that Lennon envied his ability to connect with children. This knowledge helped me shape the introductory monologue to the song "Beautiful Boy," which Lennon wrote for Sean.

One of my favorite songs in the Lennon production was "Watching the Wheels." Lennon was inspired to write this song while watching cars from his seventh-floor New York apartment window. The song was a metaphor of how humans can become like cogs in wheels. For me, this song represented Lennon's honest attempt to maintain authenticity in his extraordinary life, in which he faced constant scrutiny. I was impressed when he admitted to being anxious about parenting, a fear that many people share. I hoped that by integrating these revelations into my dialogue, others would also be touched by his life.

As you can see, I rigorously studied my source material and noted the way Lennon spoke. Then I moved beyond the facts to respectfully portray Lennon's behavior and attitudes in the context of the times. I kept the monologue for each song short. I crafted compelling information designed to inform and impact people who knew little or nothing about the final four years of Lennon's life.

Below is an example of the monologue that introduced Lennon's songs "Watching the Wheels" and "Beautiful Boy." Text in bold is verbatim speech, the words I actually heard Lennon speak. I trimmed his words down to the essentials. The rest is what I made up. My goal was to convey Lennon's dilemma: He wanted to spend time with his son, but his career also demanded attention! I wanted to reveal the intimacy he lost with his former songwriting partner Paul McCartney, who happened to be close to his own children. I also wanted show Lennon's need to "set things straight."

LENNON: *Sings* "Watching the Wheels"

LENNON: They're my own wheels, mainly. But, you know, watching meself is like watching everybody else. And I watch meself through my child, too. The thing about the child is . . . it's still hard. **I'm not the greatest dad on earth, I'm doing me best, but I get irritable, it's very hard to think about somebody else, even your own child, to really think about him.** And when I'm really thinking 'bout him, I turn it into a song! So, I write a song about the child, he's such a beautiful boy, but it would have done better for me to **spend the time I wrote the fucking song actually playing ball with my beautiful boy.** The hardest thing for me to do is play with my beautiful boy. . . . Paul was always better at it.

LENNON: *Sings* "Beautiful Boy"

Every line of dialogue has a purpose, but unlike poetry it is a means, not an end. As you write each scene, ensure that the dialogue moves the action forward.

The ancient drama device of heckling can be a useful tool for bio-dramatists. In *Barassi*, I used heckling dialogue to reveal the torment he experienced when spectators claimed he was inferior to his father. I used four hurtful lines of heckling dialogue to demonstrate what Barassi was up against when he first started playing. The following section of the script shows the rejection Barassi sometimes faced during football matches.

> *Sounds of an umpire's whistle.*
>
> *Barassi runs with the ball.*
>
> *Melbourne supporters wearing the team's scarf are in the auditorium and sit up in their seats and call out to him in anger.*

SUPPORTER 3: You're not half the footballer your dad was.

> *Barassi hesitates. The words have penetrated.*
>
> *Sounds of an umpire's whistle.*
>
> *Barassi runs again with the ball.*

SUPPORTER 1: Take off that guernsey! Barassi take off that guernsey!

SUPPORTER 2: You're only getting a game 'cause you sleep with the coach!

> *Sounds of an umpire's whistle.*
>
> *Barassi runs again with the ball and he is*

> tackled and loses the ball.
>
> Melbourne supporters sitting in the auditorium sit up in their seats and call out to him in anger.
>
>
> **SUPPORTER 3:** You're not number thirty-one and you never will be!
>
>
> Barassi is astonished and hurt. He runs off. Jack and Norm have been watching.

This dialogue allowed me, in a minute of stage time, to show through dialogue his difficult first season of football. In my research, I gathered all the insults that were hurled at him and curated them into four insults that would have been hard for him to hear and still play well. I chose each word for its power to insult and intimidate and "put off his game." This dialogue also allowed me to show a season of football in a few stage minutes.

Writing Exercises

1) *Using action to reveal subjects.* Write some actions that reveal your subject's character. You could imagine how she or he might react in different situations. Write your ideas in the form of dramatic actions, keeping in mind the subject's inner and outer goals.

2) *Knowing your subject.* The list of writing prompts below is designed to guide you toward a deeper knowledge of your character. Begin with the findings you have made in your research and then extrapolate.

> *a.* Imagine your subject talking to a family member about a personal problem. Contrast that with how the subject might talk to someone at work about the same problem. Then write some dialogue with the subject sharing the problem with a family pet.

> *b.* Write a scene in which the subject tries to return an item to a store but is refused a refund.

> *c.* Write a scene in which the character is praised for something she or he did not do.

> *d.* Write a scene that shows how the subject reacts when a friend lies.

> *e.* Write a scene in which an apparently poor and hungry stranger asks the subject for money.

3) *Ask revealing questions.* This exercise can help you integrate your research with your imagination, allowing you to write about your character's morals, beliefs, behavior, and inner conflicts. Hypothetical questions can help you decide which aspects of your character—as discovered in your research—to portray in the biographical drama. Some examples of revealing questions are:

- What uncommon beliefs does he or she have?
- What is the best thing that ever happened to your subject? The worst?
- What aspects of your subject annoy people?
- What do people like about your subject?
- What is your subject surprisingly naive about?
- What and who does your character care about the most?
- What bad habit does your character struggle to overcome?
- What does your subject deeply desire?
- How does the subject react when others are successful or get what they want?
- Where does your subject go to retreat from the world: to nature or to a bottle of whiskey?
- What is he or she anxious about?

4) *Real person to character.* What is the difference between the real character and the character that will be in your biographical drama? What choices will you need to make to portray a real person as a dramatic character? Try this exploratory exercise: Write down the names of three people you know well. Next to their names, sum them up in three words. Now expand on them: Are they witty? Cynical? Childlike? Amusing? Relaxed? Outgoing? Calm?

As an example, my partner is loving, active, and optimistic. But when I write more, I see that he is also (at times) cynical, impatient, sentimental, nostalgic. He's a serious grown-up about most things, but he has a childlike innocence on occasions. He is a scientist who poo-poos any magical thinking, but he thinks successful racehorses must have seven letters in their names. He's relaxed, until he's not. I can't easily sum my partner up. That's the point of this exercise.

Now try stating the defining traits of memorable stage and film characters. For example, MacBeth was ambitious; Lisa Simpson was smart; Frank Underwood was narcissistic; Salieri was jealous. In these cases, the dominant trait came to me more easily. So what does this tell us?

For me, it says that we can more easily see contradictions in our close family members and friends than we can see in drama characters. Many characters in drama have one defining trait, and other traits spin out from that characteristic.

Perhaps you have discovered that the subject of your biographical drama has many contradictory traits. This is where the dramatist's skill and imagination come in. You must choose the defining characteristic that will drive your drama and allow you to focus on a single trait. That focus will enable you to develop a powerful dramatic subject.

So ask yourself: With all that I know about my character, what should I choose as a dominant trait? The strongest traits are always linked to the character's deepest longing, the desire that drives his or her decisions. Macbeth realizes, after the prophesy that he will be king, that he really wants to be king! He is so deeply ambitious that he plots against and kills anyone who gets in his way.

Shakespeare based his play on the real King Macbeth of Scotland (1014-1057). Shakespeare's version of Macbeth is ambitious, but what reveals that trait? For one, he is brave. (In scene 1, Macbeth returns triumphantly from battle.) He is clever and loving. (Macbeth agrees to go along with his wife when she plots the murder of King Duncan, because he is ambitious and because he wants to please her.) He is imaginative. (Macbeth imagines life as king, but he also imagines the revengeful ghost Banquo after ordering his assassination.)

Once you have the character's defining trait, you can have a good go at expanding on the underlying motivations of his or her actions. That Macbeth wants to be king informs his character and also explains why he implements his wife's plans to kill King Duncan and then his best friend, Banquo. The deaths go on until Macbeth, blinded by ambition, meets his match and is killed.

Isolating the defining trait can help you untangle the subject's many contradictory character traits, giving your character a consistency that energizes dramatic action.

5) *Real person into character . . . into story.* Think of your subjects by adding up four things: Defining traits plus their situations, plus what they want, plus what they do to get it, equals character. Now write a sentence that sums up your character. Here's my example: Barassi's defining trait is ambition. He wants to be a footballer like his father. He defies his own physical and social limitations to succeed as a footballer, but he sacrifices his family and financial life to keep winning.

Narrative Structures and the Principles of Drama

With what you've learned about character development in mind, we turn next to the big-picture issues of writing, namely narrative structures and the principles of drama. Then, in the next chapter, we'll look at the writing process and specific ways to fine-tune your script.

Sometimes you, the writer, and you, the researcher, will feel like two different people! At first, the writer and researcher are collaborators, but eventually they must divorce (amicably). Then the writer, who has absorbed the research, emerges as the sole creator of the script. The researcher in you must always be a servant to the writer.

George Bernard Shaw's biographer, Michael Holroyd, offered an amusing take on the roles of researcher and writer:

> I think I'm two people—the researcher and the writer. The researcher spends quite a lot of time going abroad, working in libraries, seeing letters. I sometimes turn to the writer, who is doing nothing at that point—who is sleeping!—and I say, 'Do you want this bit about Shaw bicycling?' And the writer doesn't know. He says, 'You're the researcher, you decide.' So, the researcher thinks, 'Well, that's really not important.' And the researcher is always longing to be writing, getting on with the actual problem we created. Then the writer takes

over, shuts the door to the world, and kicks back on this researcher who was traveling the world, meeting people, making discoveries, and he says, 'Why the hell is there no documentation here about Shaw and the bicycle? This part of Shaw's life I show exactly about how things were happening more quickly, whereas before he was on foot.' That's what I find so funny (Cohen, 2013).

Notice that Holroyd's inner dialogue focused on what research to include or exclude from the script. For this reason, I have always kept my writer's eye open during the research phase. I like to keep the writer nearly as busy as the researcher.

Narrative Structures

One of your first writing decisions is to adopt a narrative structure, the form you will use to tell the story. Here are some choices.

Linear Chronological

This narrative structure starts at the beginning and unveils consecutive events until the finale. It is a common form in biographical drama writing that can incorporate flashbacks. The biographical drama *Unorthodox* (2020) utilizes this structure, as do many of the examples I have shared in this book.

Circular Structure

This approach is commonly employed in biographical stories. The story ends where it begins. *Iron Lady* (2011) begins with an elderly Margaret Thatcher talking to the ghost of her recently deceased husband. Then the story flashes back to her life in politics. Then there is a long midsection that covers Thatcher's twenty-five years in politics. The ending carries the audience back to the beginning, when she was elderly, and shows her still talking to her husband. This structure reveals the end and then gradually reveals how the protagonist got there. As a result of what we've learned, we interpret the end of her life differently than we did at the beginning of the film.

As with a linear chronological structure, a circular structure permits occasional flashbacks, as long as they are presented in a nonchronological sequence. Transitions between present and past (in both directions) take a lot of thought and clever construction because each scene must have some relationship to the previous scene. Writers can achieve a lot with this structure by dipping into any setting to stitch together the story.

Nonlinear or Fractured Structure

This form can be a good choice for a subject who has had a very eventful life. It can also be an effective way to portray a long period of a person's life while inviting the audience to fill in the gaps. *The Social Network* (2010) is a good example. In that film, the scenes are mostly presented as flashbacks that "interrupt" the founder of Facebook, Mark Zuckerberg, as he gives depositions in two lawsuits.

The Assassination of Gianni Versace: An American Crime Story (2018) uses a nonlinear structure to gradually show the backstory of the murderer who shot Versace in the street.

If you use this structure, make sure that the main story and the flashbacks speak to one another. The emphasis should never dwell in one place for too long because each timeline has its own merit. Each part of the story should impact the next part, causing a domino effect that moves the story forward at all times.

Parallel Structure

This structure presents two or more storylines that are tied together by an event, character, or theme. A fun example of this form is the biographical drama *Julie & Julia* (2009). Julia Child's life as a cooking teacher in the 1950s and 1960s is intertwined with blogger Julie Powell's 2002 challenge to cook within a year all the recipes in Child's first book.

Real Time

Real-time structure is tricky if the script is not short. When it's structured correctly, it can give the script a pressure-cooker intensity. I used real-time structure for my Edna Walling play. It was only forty minutes long and in the format of a guided walking tour. *Dog Day Afternoon* (1975) is a biographical drama that nearly stays in real time for the entire film. Set during a bank robbery, the real-time structure intensifies the audience experience.

David Hare's play *The Judas Kiss* (1998) is in two acts—both in real time. The first act shows the day when Irish poet and playwright

Oscar Wilde arrives at a hotel after being sentenced. His friend has arranged to whisk him away on a boat to avoid jail, but when Wilde's lover arrives, he decides to stay in England and face imprisonment. The second act is at night, years after Wilde's imprisonment, when the lover, for whom he had risked everything, betrays him.

Real-time structure is a great choice if you want to focus on a short event that changed the subject's life. Being trapped in a mine, an elevator, or a hijacked airplane are examples of situations that work well for real-time structure. However, real time works for more than just action films. It can also work for slow dramas, adding intensity, for example, to a meal during which two people fall in love (or the opposite). This structure can be powerful if the drama is about a pivotal or agonizing decision in someone's life.

The first act of *Top Girls* is presented in real time. It depicts a dinner party hosted by a contemporary woman, Marlene, who has invited women from history and fiction. The conversation reveals that their suffering has stemmed from the constraints of patriarchy. The opening real-time scene feeds subsequent acts, which occur in various timeframes. Together, the scenes follow the contemporary life, suffering, and difficulties of Marlene, who is trying to succeed in a world run by men.

Narrative Structures for Plays

Stage plays offer infinite ways to produce unconventional biographical dramas. For centuries, playwrights have used a variety of narrative devices to captivate audiences. It is helpful for writers of all genres to study plays, both ancient and modern, to gain insights about how to engage, stimulate, provoke, and delight audiences.

The earliest recorded play, at least that has survived from antiquity, was a biographical drama. Aeschylus's *The Persians* (472 BCE) dramatizes the return home of Persian King Xerxes I after a humiliating defeat. This play is fascinating because it presents the viewpoint of the losers. It is also the only Greek tragedy we have that is based on actual events that occurred at the time it was written.

Another early biographical drama titled *Octavia*, date unknown, is one of the few surviving tragedies from the Roman era. The play is about the Emperor Nero and his wife, Claudia Octavia. The six acts focus on three days in AD 62, during which Nero divorces and exiles Claudia Octavia and marries Poppaea Sabina.

Perhaps the most well-known bio-dramatist of all is William Shakespeare, who used Holinshed's *Chronicles* (1577) and Plutarch's *Lives* (first printed edition in 1470) as sources to write his plays about historical figures (Hattaway, 2003).

Historical plays provide many examples of narrative structures that can be used today. Here I want to focus on three creative strategies for developing a biographical drama structure specifically for stage presentations.

The Play within a Play

Revealing detailed information about a subject in a natural way is a skill required of all bio-dramatists. The "play within a play" approach allows playwrights to present necessary, but sometimes undramatic, biographical information in an unforced manner (exposition).

When writing a biographical drama about poet W. H. Auden,

the prolific British playwright and screenwriter Alan Bennett used the play-within-a-play framework to solve problems of exposition. Bennett had been a historian before becoming a playwright. He has since written many biographical plays and screenplays, but his primary focus has been theatrical viability, not historical accuracy. He acknowledged in his introduction to *The Madness of King George* that "one casualty of the rewrites was strict historical truth" (Bennett, 1991). He expressed concern about the variation in his audience's knowledge, which made it difficult to know what background information they would need to enjoy the play.

> As I struggle to mince these chunks of information into credible morsels of dialogue (the danger always being that characters are telling each other what they know *in their bones*). I often felt it would have been simpler to call the audience in a quarter of an hour early and give them a short curtain lecture on the nature of eighteenth-century politics before getting on with the play proper (Ibid).

Eighteen years later, Bennett was still struggling with exposition. In *The Habit of Art*, he portrays Benjamin Britten and poet W. H. Auden as artists who were not household names. Bennett admitted in the script's introduction that the play was difficult to write because there was so much information to give the audience. He partially solved this problem by having the men's actual biographer step out of the scenes to narrate.

However, Bennett's director, Nicholas Hytner, still believed that there was too much information in the play. As a result, Bennett asked to delay the play's production for a year.

> When I took [the play] up again, I found the problems to do with

too much information had not gone away, but it occurred to me that the business of conveying the facts could be largely solved if a frame were put round the play by setting it in a rehearsal room. Queries about the text and any objection to it could then be put in the mouths of the actors who (along with the audience) could have their questions answered in the course of the rehearsal (Bennett, 2009).

This play within a play device was used in another biographical drama eleven years earlier. Timberlake Wertenbaker's *After Darwin* (1998) explored the relationship between geologist Charles Darwin and Robert Fitzroy, captain of the ship *HMS Beagle*. The biographical drama begins with the staunch Christian Fitzroy clashing with the younger Darwin. When the actors step out of their roles as Darwin and Fitzroy, they reveal their struggles to survive as actors in a highly competitive industry. Thus, the primary struggle between Darwin and Fitzroy is echoed in the secondary struggle between the actors, the director, and the playwright's biographer.

Dream Frameworks

Tom Stoppard's *The Invention of Love* (1997) used a theatrical device known as "dream frameworks." This structure allowed him to caution the audience about the subjective position of the author and the imprecise nature of historical representation. The play examines the life of Alfred Edward Housman, well-known for his book of poems titled *A Shropshire Lad* (1896). Stoppard chose to examine a period in Housman's life that ranged from his student days to his last day alive. This span of fifty years is condensed into a two-hour performance. The entire play takes place in Housman's mind—while he is on his deathbed.

The dream framework frees the bio-dramatist to use biographical information at will. The advantage of this structure, said Stoppard, is that "all kinds of confusions, inaccuracies, and cheating can be attributed to the character rather than to the author" (Nadel, 2002). The audience never sees Housman sleeping, but his dream persona reveals that he is sleeping (and dreaming) in a nursing home bed.

This device also paves the way for the audience to accept, in the final scene, an elderly Housman meeting with the long-dead Oscar Wilde. (The two poets were contemporaries, but they never actually met.) The dream framework allowed the writer to faithfully portray the subject's life while also giving Housman the freedom to dramatically tell the story.

Dream frameworks also help writers cover a long span of time in a relatively short play. Flashbacks are often difficult to use in theater presentations because most dramatic tension requires a forward movement of ongoing action. Stoppard solved this problem by establishing the dream of a surreal place where the elderly protagonist watched his younger self, creating a tender poignancy to the life story.

Storytelling within Dramatic Scenes

Namatjira (Rankin, 2010) is about an indigenous Australian painter whose watercolors of central Australia introduced many Australians to their country's vast interior. The play also chronicles the life of his mentor, Rex Battarbee, a Victorian farmer and World War I veteran. Together the two men established the Hermannsburg

School for aboriginal artists.

As the play began at Sydney's Belvoir Street Theater, the audience entered while an onstage artist painted a portrait of the title actor, Trevor Jamieson. This portrait painting of Jamieson alluded to Sir William Dargie's famous Archibald Prize-winning portrait of Namatjira. Thus, by the time the play began, the audience was already immersed in a multilayered world of representation. Jamieson began to narrate the story as the artist finished his portrait. He then stepped into the set that was being painted by Namatjira's living relatives. The script also invited audience participation by training them to say hello in an indigenous language. These dramaturgical choices reminded the audience that Namatjira's story was being told from several subjective angles.

Interspersing ancient stories within European-style dramatic scenes enlightened the audience about the daily dilemmas that aboriginal artists face in their struggle to participate in two cultures. The device also provided insight into the remarkable lives and deep friendship of Namatjira and Battarbee.

Keep in mind that storytelling within dramatic scenes requires very skilled performers who have charm and dexterity. The actors must make physical and vocal adjustments to seamlessly slip in and out of time zones, places, characters, and emotional situations. They must be charismatic performers who have the skills of oral storytelling, stand-up comedy, satire, and traditional acting.

Choosing a Timeframe

Regardless of the narrative structure you choose, you will need to decide which phase of the person's life to tell. Many biographical dramas fail because the writer has included too much detail that flattens the dramatic tension. The period you choose to portray about your subject will be influenced by the themes you wish to explore.

When Peter Morgan wrote his biographical drama about Queen Elizabeth II, he chose the period soon after Princess Diana's death in a car crash. He did this to dramatize how the British Queen coped when she realized that her public response to Diana's death could save or bring down the monarchy.

Adam McKay dramatized a longer period of Dick Cheney's life, showing his younger years as a drunken, no-hope, university dropout who, with the help of a determined wife and a Machiavellian mentor, became one of the world's most powerful men.

I chose to focus on the short time that genius songwriter John Lennon spent being a househusband in New York just before he was murdered. During this phase, Lennon tussled between his profession and his desire for personal time with his second son. I focused on that phase of Lennon's life because it was not widely known. That gave me freedom to explore the tension between creativity and domesticity.

José Rivera explained to me how he chose the timeframe for the screenplay of *The Motorcycle Diaries:*

Walter Salles (the film's director) and I had many conversations about making a film about the life of Che Guevara, and Walter was convinced that Che's long life was so full of drama (personal and historical) that the only way to make a film about him would be to focus on this narrow period in his life when he took this pivotal motorcycle trip. He and I were looking for an entrance into the humanity of the man and felt that this chapter illuminated that aspect of him the best because it wasn't tainted by the fame (or infamy) he experienced later. He thought that Che before Castro was the 'purest' Che, which I agreed with.

The writer of *Judy* (2019) based on the musical *End of the Rainbow* (2005) used a circular structure, focusing on when Judy Garland was a young actress working on *The Wizard of Oz* (1939). The audience experiences the final six months of Garland's life, when she was forced to do concerts in London before her death by drug overdose at age forty-seven. The juxtaposition of these two periods provides rich insights into her tragic death.

The timeframe you choose to portray will influence casting decisions. If you select a cradle-to-grave narrative structure, you might need several actors to play the different ages of your subject. Makeup artists can age an actor, but it can be difficult for film audiences, at least, to accept an older person playing a child. In theater you can be more creative with casting. The actor who played the young Barassi also played his war-hero father. This turned out well for my final scene in which the forty-year-old Barassi met the ghost of his twenty-five-year-old father.

Age transitions in your script should naturally carry the audience forward. In season 3 of *The Crown* (2019), the actress who played Queen Elizabeth II in season 1 and 2 (Claire Foy) was too young to keep playing the older queen. To make the transition to an older actress, the writers showed a middle-age queen, played by Olivia Colman, being asked to approve a new British postage stamp that bore her profile. In the scene, the queen mentions that she now looks frumpish. A large, framed image of the new stamp appears next to an equally large image of the older stamp—a profile of a young queen, who looked like Claire Foy. Thus, the audience naturally concludes that they are seeing the same woman, only now she is more advanced in years and, yes, a little frumpish!

The Principles of Drama

Before you begin the actual writing, it will help to consider some principles of drama. It can be difficult to see the whole story played out in your head during the research process, but thinking about the principles of drama can help you envision the elements of your biographical drama. These principles are set out below.

The Initiating Incident

The initiating incident sets the story in motion. It may not be seen onstage or onscreen, but it will drive the story. This incident must be sufficiently powerful, so powerful that the story couldn't have been made without it. In *The King's Speech*, the initiating incident was King George's brother's abdication of the crown. Had that not occurred, George's stutter wouldn't have mattered as much. In the case of *Barassi*, he would not have been so driven to succeed if his father had not died as a football star and war hero.

In *Unorthodox* (2020), the initiating incident was the lead character being taken from her mother as a young child and being told that the mother had abandoned her. We do not learn about this until near the end of the drama.

Establishment of the Status Quo

All drama requires audiences to understand the main character's normal life. For audiences to understand what is at stake for your character, they need the writer to show them what typical life was like before the drama begins. In *The King's Speech,* Bertie's normal was to serve as a naval officer, and be a happy husband and father who quietly struggled with a stutter. Barassi's normal was his happy family life and his football world. Esty in *Orthodox* (2020) is lovingly raised by her orthodox Jewish grandmother.

Interruption of the Status Quo

This dramatic principle involves setting up the main conflict of the story. It includes a "call to action," something that must be done to remedy a problem or crisis. Bertie the naval officer is forced to become the king; therefore, he must confront his inability to speak in public. Barassi's mother has to move, which separates her son from his football club and forces him to choose between his family and his passion. Esty must leave her orthodox community when she realizes she and her baby will be outcasts forever.

The Protagonist's Goal

The protagonist must have a clear goal. The king seeks to overcome his stammer. Barassi strives to be the best at football. Esty pursues a new life in Berlin. These protagonists each had inner goals that were at odds with their outer goals.

Obstacles

As protagonists pursue their goals, they often face major obstacles. At first the king couldn't find a good speech therapist. When he found the Australian therapist, the king had to learn humility and trust before he could improve. As the king and therapist worked through the obstacles, they learned something about themselves. Barassi learned that his methods to win at all costs eventually stopped working. Esty found herself broke and alone in a strange country, her dreams of getting a scholarship dashed.

Complications

Life is complicated, so show your character grappling with nagging problems. These complications can increase the intensity of your drama. The king's life grew more complicated when people pressured him to not trust the person who had most helped him overcome his stutter. Then the king heard that his speech therapist had no qualifications. Barassi returned to football and had more success, but when he returned to his father's club, his coaching techniques failed. The more intensely Barassi tried to impose his techniques, the worse his team played. Other areas of his life also failed. Esty escaped to Berlin but her mother did not answer the door and she ended up homeless.

Crisis

All the action of a drama leads to the *crux,* the moment of crisis. By now in the performance, audiences should be in tune with this moment. We want to know! Will the king do the national radio speech without the therapist who had helped him? How will Barassi go on after a devastating failure at his father's club? Will Esty go back to her husband who promised to change?

Climax

This is the tensest part of a play or film. The king defied his people and, with the speech therapist's help, made a near-perfect, nationally broadcast speech. Barassi met the ghost of his father and understood that winning was not the most important thing in life; rather, living a good, long life, which his father couldn't attain, became more important. Esty hugged her husband after he cut off his payots (the curled side locks of hair mandated by the ultra-orthodox community) to prove to her that he would change—a moment when we feel hearts breaking.

Obligatory Scene

Another dramatic principle to consider, which can be part of the climax, is the obligatory or controlling scene. It most often occurs near the end of a play or film, like the shootout at the end of a Western film. The initiating incident (see above) sets up the obligatory scene. In *Barassi*, the initiating incident is the death of Barassi's war-hero father in Tobruk. The obligatory scene occurs when Barassi goes to his father's grave and talks with him. In *The King's Speech*, the initiating incident occurs when Prince Albert (Bertie) gives a humiliating public speech with a strong stammer. The obligatory scene happens when he gives an empowering speech as king while his nation is at war. In both works, the inciting incident predisposes the audience to receive the obligatory scene.

You have to be careful to not make the relationship of these two scenes too obvious or formulaic. Bio-dramatist Jeff Pope's *Stan and Ollie* (2018) presents the initiating incident early in the film. The two comedians are at the height of their careers, but cash-strapped Ollie refuses to join Stan's rejection of an unfair Hollywood contract (which screws over Stan's career). The obligatory scene arrives as expected near the end of the film when the two men have reunited to successfully tour England. Pope managed to rise above cliché by infusing the scene with powerful emotions.

I know I have a strong structure for my biographical drama scripts when I can see a solid idea for an obligatory scene that reflects the purpose of the whole story and fulfills the audience's expectations. In *The Motorcycle Diaries* (2003), the initiating incident is cleverly placed in the middle of the film. Guevara and his travelling companion share a meal with an evicted, penniless couple who are searching for the only work they can find in the dangerous mines of Chile. Guevara and his companion are forced to see their own privilege when the destitute couple asks them if they, too, are travelling to find work. The young men realize that they are among the "haves" in an increasingly unequal society. This scene sets up the penultimate scene, near a leper colony, in which the asthmatic Guevara swims across a dangerous river that divides the medical staff from the lepers. This scene displays his nascent inner goal to break the divide between the sick and the healthy, between the haves and the have nots. This scene enables the audience to understand the meaning of the story and to gain insight into Guevara's heart and mind.

In *Collette* (2018), the protagonist must confront her husband and declare independence from his control and society's tyranny. Stan and Ollie must have a full-blown ugly fight in public to purge the long-term simmering resentment between them. *The Lehman Trilogy* shows the company's spiral into financial devastation. In episode 7 of *The Crown* (2019), Prince Phillip must return to face the group of burned-out priests to confess his mid-life crisis and his need for help.

It will help you to structure your biographical drama if you work out the obligatory scene early in the writing process. I decided that the obligatory scene in *Barassi* would be the second-to-last scene in which Barassi meets his dead father. I knew that I had to prime the audience early, so I added an early scene of the young father going to war.

Skilled bio-dramatists can play with audience expectations by delaying the obligatory scene for as long as possible or by presenting it in an original way. A good example of the first is *Collete* (2018). She attempts to live an authentic life as an artist, but she is repeatedly thwarted by her opportunistic husband. She, at last, explosively forces him out of her life and out of her writing career. For *Stan and Ollie,* the writer established early the tension between the two ageing comics by showing how Stan stayed with the studio instead of joining Ollie as a freelancer, thus railroading Ollie's career. Late in the movie, the two of them confront the reasons for that devastating break-up.

Sometimes the desire for a powerful obligatory scene can override historical accuracy. Schiller's *Mary Stuart* (1800) imagined a scene between Elizabeth I and Mary Queen of Scots that never took place. The audience wanted to see the two women battle it out.

Consider audience expectations if you are writing an obligatory scene about someone famous. Jockey Michelle Payne must have her Melbourne Cup victory. Napoleon, his Waterloo. Neil Armstrong, his walk on the moon.

Lagos Egri described the obligatory scene this way: "But one chain on a link that encompasses the whole play. There is an accumulative power that drives the drama forward so that while the final conflict may mark the end of the story, it is on one level simply repeating in greater intensity what the audience has been experiencing throughout the drama" (Egri, 1946).

Resolution

Resolution ties up all the loose ends. It gives us a glimpse of the future. The king was cured. The football star was no longer haunted. The restless young man knows what he must do with his life. The prince walks with the priests through the garden as his concerned wife, the queen, watches with a smile. As Esty waits in a Berlin café, her compass points to the new musician friends who join her.

The Power of a Good Ending

A good way to end this chapter is to focus on how to end a biographical drama. Generally, the critical acts in a biographical drama occur five minutes before the end. Audiences need time to take in the climax, feel themselves to be within the spell of the narrative, and then to be led out of it.

The script's ending must reveal the biographical drama's central meaning. A classic example from literature would be Nora leaving her marriage in the final scene of Ibsen's *The Doll's House* (1889). Nora's outer goal is to save her marriage, but by the end of the play she realizes the marriage isn't worth saving. Her goal changes: to save her own life by leaving the marriage.

American dramatist David Mamet writes the following about how to end a play:

> At that point, then, in the well-wrought play (and perhaps in the honestly examined life) we will understand that what seemed accidental was essential, we will perceive the pattern wrought by our character, we will be free to sigh or mourn. And then we can go home (Mamet, 1998).

My biographical drama *Barassi* concludes with he and his second wife planning a future together. He was finally free from the haunting pressure to be better than his father. My play about Edna Walling concludes with Edna leaving the garden she had designed, fully satisfied with her legacy, and moving on to another garden. At the end of *Amadeus,* Salieri is incarcerated in a mental asylum. He tells the inmates that he would be the patron saint of mediocrity. As the film ends, he hears Mozart's annoying laughter. Charles Kane, on his death bed, grasps a snow dome and utters his final word—Rosebud—the name of his childhood sled, which he loved to play with as an innocent worry-free child. In *Judy*, the titular character sings her most famous song, "Somewhere Over the Rainbow," but breaks down as she realizes that, for her, there is nothing over the rainbow. Her audience finishes the song for her.

Writing Exercises

1) *Finding the conflict.* Based on your research, identify a scenario in your subject's life that involved conflict. Did your subject experience a time when he or she was distrusted, or lost something valuable, or battled inner demons, or was treated unfairly? Write for twenty minutes about that conflict. You might want to repeat this exercise for each of the dramatic principles outlined in this chapter. They are:

- The Initiating Incident
- Establishment of the Status Quo
- Interruption of the Status Quo
- The Protagonist's Goal
- Obstacles
- Complications
- Crisis
- Climax
- The Obligatory Scene
- Resolution

2) *Finding the narrative structure.* Is there a dramatic arc to your subject's life story? Have you found the best narrative structure to present that story? As Peter Arnott states: "Finding the shape of the life gives you the shape of your play" (author's interview, 2016). He revealed a shape to Joplin's life by emphasizing how differently she behaved at two separate concerts, one early in her career and one at the end of her life. Spend some time writing your thoughts about the arc of the subject's life.

CHAPTER 9

Elements of the Writing Process

Now that we have studied character development, narrative structures, and the basic principles of drama, we can turn our attention to the writing process. This chapter focuses on how to approach the writing process while fine-tuning and intensifying your script.

The Actor As a Writing Collaborator

As bio-dramatists begin to write, they often overlook the importance of the lead actor's role in developing the script. In *Performing History* (2000), Freddie Rokem asserted that the actor becomes a "hyper-historian." The actor brings the historical past and the theatrical present together (Rokem, 2000) as a living representation of the subject, thereby presenting both performer and dramatist with opportunities and limitations not relevant or available to the prose biographer. As Rokem suggests, this should be seen as a source of authorization for the bio-dramatist, perhaps more so than historical accuracy. "Theater performing history takes over the role of the professional historian," said Rokem, "but instead of relying on documents or other biographical sources, theater relies on the actors' ability to convince the spectators that something from the real historical past has been presented on the stage (Ibid).

Collaboration between writer and actor during the writing process is usually invisible, but nevertheless real. For example, as I wrote *Barassi,* I imagined my actor giving the famous halftime speech to the players in the Grand Final of 1972. This helped me give both actor and audience a dramatic connection to the speech, which occurred decades earlier. Imagining the actor enabled me to write so that audiences would experience being in a locker room at the Melbourne Cricket Ground (where the football finals were held). No prose biography can offer that experience! Although the actor wasn't physically present when I wrote the scene, he shaped my writing.

Bio-dramatists, unlike prose historians, can leverage the power of actors to connect the historical past with fictional present as they write, making the events seem more real. The three-dimensional nature of theater, and the two dimensions of film, place audiences in close proximity with the biographical subject. This lends an immediacy to the experience and allows actors to gain the audience's acceptance.

My experience aligns with Rokem's assertion that actors take some of the weight of writing from the writer's shoulders. A good actor helps the writer win the acceptance of audiences. Actor Jeremy Irons, who played former British Prime Minister Harold MacMillan in *Never So Good* (Brenton, 2008), alluded to this when he described his approach to performing a real person: "This is MacMillan. Forget what you know or how I look—because I don't look like him. This is him" (Cantrell and Luckhurst, 2010).

The quest to convince audiences is central to the bio-dramatist's work. In order for an audience to accept the narrative, the bioramatist and the actor-historian need to successfully appeal for the audience's belief in a way that goes beyond the normal request for their suspension of disbelief. That's because audiences bring their own preconceptions with them to a biographical drama.

José Rivera believes that biographical dramas should be an experience as opposed to a lesson; that is, to engage with characters in a visceral way. When writers write to that end, they can more easily translate a script into action. In Rivera's play about Che Guevara's last two days, Che is tied up in a schoolroom while a young schoolteacher feeds him soup. "When they eat the soup together, it's a very sexy moment," said Rivera, "because his arms are tied and she's right in his face putting the soup in his mouth and he's sucking it down and the two actors really make a moment of it and that's what I want—I want those experiences as opposed to a factual understanding of Che. I want the visceral understanding."

How can you write so that an actor can give audiences a visceral understanding of your subject's life? The script must convince good actors that the material will support them sufficiently for their biographical portrayal. Simon Callow shared his frustration about playing Mozart in the premier production of *Amadeus* (1980). Callow's research revealed that there was more to the musician than Peter Shaffer, the playwright, had included in the script. Shaffer had to be firm, reminding Callow that his script was about "Mozart as remembered by Salieri." Callow was forced to find the truth inside Shaffer's "partial picture of Mozart" (Cantrell and Luckhurst, 2010). So, the pressure is on the writer to get the script right, to support the actor's efforts and to engage the audience.

Consider Your Audience

As you write the first draft, I encourage you to think judiciously about your audience's expectations and perceptions. We discussed this matter earlier in the book, but it is important to briefly mention again now that you are about to write.

After substantial research on *Barassi,* I had learned a lot about my subject (and about myself). However, I realized that I needed to get outside myself and carefully review audience perceptions about Barassi, which I had gleaned from my *vox populi* surveys. A play about a well-known figure such as Barassi would draw a different audience than the kind of people who typically attend a fictional play. Many of them would have preconceived expectations and a lot of historical knowledge about him. Fortunately, I saw a natural alignment between the dramatic narrative I had in mind and the perspectives that people shared with me about Barassi. But if I had neglected to think about my audience's viewpoint, I could have produced a flop.

Ursula Canton's scholarly research about biographical theater adds weight to my point. In her book *Biographical Theatre,* she claimed that after-play conversations about biographical works differ from those that follow fictional dramas. Audiences, theater reviewers, and practitioners comment less about the *quality* of biographical dramas and more about how writers and actors portray real subjects. Many reviewers measure performances against their prior knowledge about the subject. Canton concludes: "Practitioners and audiences would see and interpret biographical performances differently from performances that did not have such a close link to the life world through comparison with previous discourses about the historical characters" (Canton, 2009).

In other words, audience perceptions about the subject influence how they receive the work. Your audience might go see your biographical drama because they have a strong interest in and familiarity with your subject. Therefore, you must not be presumptuous about an audience's knowledge about that person, especially if he or she is famous.

As I mentioned earlier, my play about Edna Walling was performed in one of her famous gardens as part of an Open Garden day. I knew there would be people in my audience who might know more than I did about Walling. But I also had to deal with people who knew nothing about her. To help solve this problem, I had a fictional character pretend to be a bossy tour guide who, while giving a rundown on Walling's life, was interrupted and corrected by the ghost of Edna Walling. Her ghost was more interested in what people were doing in gardens today than talking about her past. This approach allowed me to reveal the right amount of biographical facts while also presenting a passionate drama about how designing a garden can impact one's soul. I was also able to obliquely demonstrate Walling's considerable legacy.

Suspense, Humor, and Time

There are several other factors to consider as you write. They are related to the principles of drama, but distinct enough to highlight here.

Dramatic Energy: Creating Suspense

You should look for opportunities to give your scenes suspense and surprise. Alfred Hitchcock, the king of suspense, explained the difference between suspense and surprise. Say you write a scene with people at a table and suddenly, *boom*, a bomb goes off. You've created surprise. By contrast, if you write about a person who arrives and places the bomb under the table before people sit down, you have created suspense.

A scene in *The Assassination of Gianni Versace: An American Crime Story* (2018) shows the central character, Andrew Cunanan, just after he murders his first victim and is holding David Madson hostage in David's apartment. When David's friend and the building superintendent come looking for him and hear something behind the door, they immediately get the master key. We perceive that Cunanan has only a short period of time to escape with his hostage. However, the writer fudged the facts to create suspense. Police reports stated that hours passed before the initial knock and the opening of the door.

To increase tension, you might allow audiences to know something your protagonist doesn't. Horror films often use this tactic. For example, audiences might know that a psychotic killer is lurking around a corner as an unsuspecting character approaches. Another device to intensify a biographical drama is to put your character under the force of time. You have permission to stretch the facts here! Freddie Mercury and his band had only days to rehearse for Live Aid. Stutterer Prince Albert's speech to the nation had to be ready by a deadline—his coronation as the new King of England!

Leaving Clues about Your Subject

You can add texture to a biographical drama by leaving clues about daily, routine aspects of your subject. You can base these clues on what you find in research or by using your informed imagination. You might show how the person ties his shoelaces, undresses before bed, pats a dog, looks at himself in a mirror, or packs for a trip. Does he pack books, snacks, alcohol, or a portrait of his cat? Think about ways you can reveal interesting aspects of your character in ways that are less literal.

Finding Humor

Even when experiencing serious biographical dramas, audiences enjoy seeing the funny side of characters. In *Dog Day Afternoon,* Sonny Wortzik is an amateurish criminal. When he robs a bank, his gun gets stuck in a bag. A scene in which Barassi is angry at his footy players because they played badly, he kicks a wall and breaks his toe; the players, once intimidated, now can't help but laugh. In *Red Joan,* the elderly British woman accused of spying for Russia serves tea in mugs emblazoned with images of the revolutionary Che Guevara. In *Stan and Ollie,* the writers included a scene in which Stan keeps falling over his suitcases in a hotel lobby. The humor stems from the fact that Stan is a world-famous slapstick comedian. In *Vice,* dark humor emerges when the waiter offers a menu of constitutional grey areas, including torture and rendition. Dick Cheney, Donald Rumsfeld, and others in the film have been exploiting the grey areas to gain what they wanted. Cheney orders everything on the menu.

As you write humor into your script, be careful to maintain a sympathetic tone. Making nasty fun of your character will not often be received well by audiences.

Dramatic Time

Life can be long, but biographical dramas are time dependent. As writers, we expect audiences to sit quietly and watch a story. Therefore, the drama we write must hold their attention for the duration of the presentation. Time factors often play a role in the use of dramatic license. So how do we compress a real-life event that might have taken months or years into tight scenes?

Ironically, audiences might criticize a biographical drama that remains faithful to the facts if the work fails to engage them. If you are determined to completely show a long-term real event, you could frustrate audiences. People are interested in what your subject did, but they are *engaged* by gaining insight into your subject's motivations and goals. We watch biographical dramas to understand what makes a person tick, to experience the subject's life at a safe distance. Audiences want an emotional connection. This means the writer must find a way to compress time. How?

Barassi took weeks to decide whether to leave his father's football club to play for a much-hated rival team. In the 1950s, Barassi's departure from his father's club shocked the football world. Over the course of months, he publicly changed his mind several times. If I had portrayed all those inconvenient details, I would have diluted the drama. So, I wrote a scene in which his agonizing decision was reached within just a few pages of the script—a seven-minute scene. Similarly, bio-dramatist Gavin Hood discovered that it took six editorial meetings at *The Observer* before the newspaper's editors decided to print the leaked memo that was central to *Official Secrets* (2019*)*. Hood contracted all of those meetings into one tense encounter.

In *Bohemian Rhapsody* (2018), the subject, Freddie Mercury, stumbled into a 1970 performance by Brian May and Roger Taylor's band, which was called Smile before it was changed to Queen. Mercury met with May and Taylor after the show, coincidentally right after their bassist/singer Tim Staffell quit. May and Taylor were skeptical of Mercury at first, but he won them over when he delivered an impromptu rendition of their song "Doing Alright."

In reality, Mercury (far less dramatically) met his future band while attending Ealing Art College in London. The made-up scene nicely compressed time and information.

In *The King's Speech*, Bertie (King George VI) met with Lionel, the progressive speech therapist, just before he became king. Actually, Lionel had worked with then-Prince Bertie decades before Bertie's brother famously abdicated to marry his mistress. The timing of the speech lessons was shifted and concentrated to give the film more emotional power and a more satisfying dramatic shape.

Facts might shift, but the story remains real. Some facts are easier to shift than others. Changing dates and locations are fine in a story about a singer or even a king from a previous century. But if you shift the date of the winning goal scored by your subject during a memorable game, you will probably alienate your audiences.

A biographical drama that failed with time compression and artistic license was *Grace of Monaco* (2014). Many critics said that the writer overly exaggerated the diplomatic scandal between France and Monaco in order to increase the drama. The writer also asked audiences to accept that Grace Kelly had found her princess mojo while fighting for her new country to remain a tax-free zone. A script that asks people to side with tax evaders doesn't always go down well. The lesson? Your invention or amplification of facts must remain plausible and enjoyable. Therefore, be judicial with how you shift the facts!

Two Writing Processes

With these elements of biographical drama writing in mind, you can determine how you will approach the writing process. What works best depends on each person's creative style, but most writers use one of two common plans. My intent is not to limit you to one or the other, as you might have had success with your own style. You also might find it natural to blend the two that I discuss in this chapter.

The first approach starts with *conception,* then moves to *incubation,* and then to *production.* The writer starts with conceptual thinking and hopes that a dramatic form will organically emerge in her or his mind. Pulitzer Prize-winning playwright Edward Albee would go for long walks on the beach over a period of months until he had his play fully formed in his mind. His scripts emerged after months of thinking, dreaming, and trying out the whole story in his head. When a hen incubates an egg, she waits for the fully formed chick to break through the shell. Similarly, the drama's framework is fully incubated before the writer does the actual writing (production).

The other common writing process starts with *prewriting,* then moves to actual *writing,* and finally to *rewriting.* During the prewriting phase, the writer spends a lot of time with exploratory writing. Prewriting helps some writers find a dramatic framework (a concept) while also helping them to put creative ideas on paper. Then, during the writing phase, the writer pieces it all together into a rough draft. Rewriting involves transforming the rough draft into a strong dramatic shape.

This writing process is rather recursive. An initial pathway forward promotes an intuitive flow of energy and then carries the script through multiple iterations. The process is not as linear as the process of conception, incubation, and production.

Both processes have merit. You can choose one (or blend them) based on your own preferences. However, you should bring some order to the writing process and avoid a haphazard approach.

Creative Outlining

Regardless of which writing process to use, the narrative structure (see the previous chapter) of your script will determine where you begin and end. As Arnott suggested, when you choose the shape of a life, you are presenting your argument for what that person's life means to you.

So, after you've chosen your narrative structure and considered which writing process to employ, you can use creative outlining to translate those concepts into the actual script.

The term *outlining* often conjures unpleasant memories of eighth-grade essay classes, but it can be a central element of the creative process. Writing an outline helps you fit the specifics of the biographical drama into a preconceived framework. Rivera says that outlining bridges research and writing. It is a vital part of "wrighting" and writing your script.

When crafting an outline, you begin the profound process of choosing what to exclude and include in the story—decisions that are often not easy to make. When asked what information she extracted from her research to write about singer Edith Piaf and painter Stanley Spencer, British playwright Pam Gems responded this way: "You just take what you want to service your play's themes" (Stephenson and Langridge, 1998). For her, "drama is a practical craft, shaped and sometimes released by exigency" (Ibid). In other words, you obtain information about your subject and then use the outline to shape a good story that is based on your research.

The artistic freedom to leave certain facts behind means that bio-dramatists set their own parameters for telling a life story. Writing the outline is, essentially, the creative element of choosing what to leave behind.

Scottish scriptwriter Peter Arnott, who wrote a play about singer Janice Joplin, told me that outlining is the act of "finding the shape of the life." He believes that writing an outline enables the writer to see the shape the person's life. Finding the shape of the life gives you the shape of your script. One shape can map onto the other. In Arnott's words:

> When you are making an argument about what someone's life might signify, what it might mean, . . . the overall superstructure of that must, has to, come from that shape—you make the shape and that's your argument, that's your case. It means you are in the happy position where the structure of your play makes your argument. It's grounded in what really happened. Of course, you make stuff up—

once you've found your shape (personal interview, 2016).

Arnott displayed the shape of Joplin's life in his biographical drama titled *Full Tilt* (2014) after he found one of her last concerts on YouTube. She spoke a monologue between songs. He decided to frame his first act between two monologues. The first is upbeat as she talks about man-hunting in San Francisco, but the final monologue is a desperate, heart-breaking plea for love that reveals her sadness. The final monologue finishes with her singing "Ball and Chain."

I found the shape of *Barassi* when I discovered that his drive to be the best was propelled by his desire to live up to his hero father. The scenes were all designed to serve this idea. Other interesting things that Barassi did with his life were left out.

So, the outlining stage is your response to the life you're writing about. The outline will reveal what that person's life meant to you. Screenwriter Akiva Goldsman spoke about outlining his biographical script for *A Beautiful Mind* (2001):

> The outline phase is interminable but essential. Since this is a story about a mathematician, perhaps this is as close to math as the writing process comes. You must work your way through the mechanics and break the back of the story before you can proceed to putting words on paper. All the great dialogue in the world won't save you if the story structure isn't there (*Script Magazine*, 2012).

Many writers produce forty-page outlines before they begin to write the script. They need to "see" the story play out. Here is the beginning of an outline I wrote for a screenplay about Australian animal welfare activist Lyn White.

EXT. COFFEE SHOP, EVENING

Lyn is dressed in a designer dress. She stops to look at a dog tied to a post outside the coffee shop. The dog is shaking with its tail between its legs. Lyn is pulled away by her assistant who has her lecture notes.

EXT. DOORWAY OF CONFERENCE CENTER

Lyn is surrounded by people in Animal Liberation tee-shirts. Behind them are posters of farm animals in horrific conditions. They marshal her inside the conference center as they try to shield Lyn from farmers and from the meat farmers' lobby who have managed to enter the center. They direct her to a back entrance.

INT. LARGE CONFERENCE ROOM, EVENING

Lyn walks onto the stage with a powerful upright walk and a small smile as the audience stands and applauds her. Flashes of images: the shaking dog, the frightened farm animals, and the angry farmers make her hesitate before she begins her lecture.

I find that outlining is a great way to get all your mental images onto the page. It can give you a better idea of whether the story is engaging and plausible. Some people use index cards for each scene and pin them on the wall. I remember having trouble with the structure of one of my plays, so I wrote all the scenes down on index cards and then pinned them up on a line, like laundry, and literally walked along the play. That helped me see the overall structure and where it was lacking.

You can also use a bullet-point sketch. Below is the outline I wrote for *Barassi*.

- Father winning the 1940 Grand Final and then leaving as a soldier for Tobruk

- Child kicking the ball under the line of trees planted in honor of his dead father
- Not a natural, but determined to be as good as he can be
- Norm Smith's ongoing anguish over Barassi senior leading him to encourage his son
- His mother remarrying and wanting to go to Tasmania, far from his father's club
- The fight to live with Norm Smith and play for his father's club
- Being ungainly, not quite fitting until Norm invents a position
- Discovering his superpower when let loose as a Ruck / Rover
- Becoming vice captain
- Getting married young to please Norm Smith
- The 1958 Grand Final that crushes dreams
- Captain Rambunctious
- Getting older and being offered a coaching job at another club
- Will he or won't he leave his father's club?
- Carlton Football Club and loyalty
- Bolstering the battling Blues (Blues are the Carlton Football Club)
- Winning in 1960
- Sick of football
- Being a civilian (Barassi very publicly retires from football)
- Back in the game with the Roos (the North Melbourne Football Club)
- Life falling apart (divorce and bankruptcy as he wins in 1972)

- Returning to redeem his father's club
- Meeting his bohemian second wife and losing at his father's club
- Defeated, he needs to see the only person who could heal him
- The military graveyard at Tobruk, meeting his dead father
- Ghost soldiers playing Australian football
- Epilogue

This outline revealed to me a full, eventful life held in the public eye, and it helped me avoid presenting too much information in relation to stage time. The screenwriting guru, Robert McKee, said that to "tell a story that spans a lifetime, a spine of enormous power and persistence must be created" (McKee, 1999). He added that events must be linked in a meaningful way by "a single, deep desire, aroused out of an inciting incident in childhood that must go unquenched for decades" (Ibid). Barassi had this deep, single desire, which helped me choose events to include in my play. As I developed the outline, his desire to please his father gave my script that "spine."

Despite the benefits of outlines, not all dramatists like to use them. Harold Pinter believes that writing an outline can hamper the imagination and suppress surprise discoveries (Royal Court talk, 1998). By jumping straight in and writing the script, some writers discover their characters in the moment of writing. Perhaps these writers, like Pinter, have a powerful sense of innate dramatic structure that we mere mortals lack. Most of us need to conceptualize, free write, and outline scripts to avoid a lot of revision.

Forward Movement

Once the outline is completed, make sure that you have allowed for forward movement. Specifically, consider what conditions you have established in each scene that will propel your audience into the next. That your subject did remarkable things is not enough. The facts must be presented in dramatic form. The audience needs to feel like they are on a journey through your subject's life. Their hearts must beat faster as they move toward the subject's fate.

The first scenes in the biographical drama *Shadowlands* (1993), about British writer C.S. Lewis, establish Lewis as a committed bachelor with a routine life as a professor. The scene in which he meets an American pen pal, poet Joy Gresham, surprises him. As they continue to meet, a strong connection develops between the two writers. When the connection threatens to become romantic, Lewis resists. Drama can spring from a character's resistance to change. The meetings between Lewis and Gresham display how their intellects, wit, and spiritual paths are *simpatico*. Scene by scene, the script gently makes it clear that they are falling in love, by layering their slowly eroding resistances to change. Resistance to love eventually leads them to part ways—only to rejoin later.

Are the layers of change in your character's life apparent in each scene? Each scene should have its own arc, but each should yield something unresolved in order to energize movement toward the next scene. Obstacles, in most cases, need to be progressive.

Forward movement can also be established by revealing stressful relationships. In *Amadeus* (1984), Salieri loves God, but because God has granted him less talent than Mozart, he wonders if God loves *him*. This tension between Salieri and God propels the scenes forward.

Karen Blixen, in the film *Out of Africa* (1985), arrives in Africa with the belief that she is defined by her possessions. By the end of the film, her experiences have changed her. She comes to see that she should be defined by her values and actions. This helps her grieve the sudden death of her lover and the loss of her farm and coffee plantation. By surrendering all—her wayfaring husband, her loyal servants, her farm in Africa—she gains her true self. This process of change carries the scenes forward in a compelling, personal manner.

Merging Characters

Through the course of life, people can accumulate a few dozen major relationships. In a biographical drama, however, the people in the main subject's life often need to be amalgamated. Audiences can only relate to a limited number of people, especially in a short time.

Bio-dramatist John Logan successfully combined characters in his play about painter Mark Rothko in *Red* (2009). The play focused on the period when Rothko was commissioned to paint a series of works for an expensive Manhattan restaurant, The Four Seasons. Rothko had dozens of assistants throughout his career, each for short periods of time. For the play, Logan created one fictional assistant, Ken, who stayed with Rothko for two years while Rothko painted his Seagram series.

Barassi coached hundreds of football players. I judiciously melded them into three significant relationships that I used to theatrically display the blind spots in Barassi's ambition. I chose Alex Jesaulenko, because he was a family man who wanted a life-work balance that Barassi couldn't contemplate, let alone achieve. I selected Syd Jackson because he was famous for his cheekiness and humor, which upset Barassi at training sessions. I also included Brent Crosswell, an intellectual and philosophical man who quoted Homer and other poets in response to Barassi's outbursts. The three players displayed the important attributes Barassi lost to his blind ambition: family life, a sense of humor, and a philosophical outlook.

The Australian biographical drama *Shine* (1996), about concert pianist David Helfgott, depicted Helfgott's powerful, antagonistic father responding to his early musical success with fierce competitiveness and brutal repression. This led to the pianist's mental health problems. As a middle-age and homeless man, Helfgott met a positive form of antagonism in his wife, who helped him overcome his inner demons and perform in a well-received comeback concert.

Subjects who are leaders, such as teachers and coaches, have often influenced many lives, so you will need to choose important subsidiary characters and combine them. I recommend watching biographical dramas such as *Freedom Writers* (2007) and *The Damned United* (2009) to see examples of how supporting actors can be amalgamated. Check your biographical drama to see if your subsidiary characters are interesting sources of antagonism (both positive and negative), people who help reveal more about your main character.

Writing Exercises

1) *Unearthing your subconscious.* The creative process of writing a biographical drama is inextricably linked to your subconscious. So, spend some time free writing. You might end up using all or some of the free writing in your script, but the point is to work your writing "muscles," to remember your research, and to enable your subconscious to rise to the surface. Free writing is the time to find *your* story within the framework of your subject's story—without censor!

To get the most out of this exercise, don't think before you write. Just start writing. You can write fast or slow but don't cross anything out or fix spelling. Follow your energy. Work in a quiet, uninterrupted place and write anything about your biographical drama for thirty minutes. I sometimes like to free write with another writer buddy who honors the rules.

2) *Study outlines of IMDb.com.* If you would like some extra inspiration to write your outline, go to IMDb.com, the Internet Movie Database, and look at TV or movies. I enjoy looking at biographical drama series such as *The Crown, American Crime Story,* or *Orthodox* for good plotting, dramatic tension, escalating conflict, etc. Choose a film or a season. Click on plot summary and you will find a brief plot summary or the full synopsis. For extra insight, view the episode or film and study how the outline became a strong script.

CHAPTER 10

Rewriting, Feedback, and Public Readings

You have written your first draft. That is a big achievement. I always give myself some time to enjoy this accomplishment, so give yourself a treat. Of course, there is work to be done, but do enjoy this milestone and have a short break before you reread your first draft. Most first drafts are fledgling. Rewriting is a natural part of the writing process.

It also requires humility. You must confess (at least to yourself) that your first draft is not good enough, even though you are by now deeply attached to your script—as parents to a newborn child.

William Zinsser, in his classic book titled *On Writing Well,* says this about rewriting:

> Rewriting is the essence of writing well: It's where the game is won or lost. That idea is hard to accept. We all have an emotional equity in our first draft; we can't believe that it wasn't born perfect. But the odds are close to 100 percent that it wasn't. . . . I've never thought of rewriting as an unfair burden; I'm grateful for every chance to keep improving my work (Zinsser, 2001).

Writer Anne Lamott, in her book titled *Bird by Bird: Some Instructions on Writing and Life,* had this to say about rewriting and revising:

I know some very great writers, writers you love who write beautifully and have made a great deal of money, and . . . not one of them writes elegant first drafts. All right, one of them does, but we do not like her very much. . . . For me and most of the other writers I know, writing is not rapturous. In fact, the only way I can get anything written at all is to write really, really shitty first drafts. The first draft is the child's draft, where you let it all pour out and then let it romp all over the place, knowing that no one is going to see it and that you can shape it later (Lamott, 1995).

Stephen King (yes, *that* Stephen King), learned the value of rewriting when he was in high school. The editor of his town's weekly newspaper, a man named John Gould, gave King the opportunity to write articles about local sports. When King turned in his first two articles, Gould started marking one of them up with a black pen, mostly nixing unnecessary words. Then Gould told King, "When you write a story, you're telling yourself the story. When you rewrite, your main job is taking out all the things that are *not* the story" (King, 2000).

Once you've found the biographical drama's shape then you need to eliminate everything else that is not part of that shape. As I said, rewriting a script requires humility. And if you're not humble, if you think that your first draft is good, then your biographical drama probably won't be.

However, most of the professional writing guides I've read seem to assume that we know what will make a revision better. Do we? Those writing guides don't offer much guidance about what makes second or third drafts "good." Just because someone is humble enough to revise and rewrite doesn't mean that the final product will be better. We need some criteria to guide our revision efforts.

In this chapter, I provide some criteria for revising a biographical drama. They are not meant to be restrictive, but to give you reference points for what makes biographical dramas great. With these in mind, rewriting won't feel like being lost in a forest without a compass. I'll also provide you with a helpful step-by-step process for working on second and third drafts. Hopefully, the chapter will enable you, like a sculptor, to hack off all the rough edges of the script and reveal the magnificent story inside.

Criteria for Script Revision

Start each rewrite with a purpose and look carefully at your first draft by examining each of the criteria shown in this section of the chapter. You might be able to evaluate all the factors in one reading, but I find it helpful to read through the script numerous times with just one factor in mind. As you evaluate your work, I recommend rewriting the sections that need to be adjusted, according to the criteria below.

Structure and Mechanics

Start by looking at the overall structure and mechanics of the script. The first act is the set-up, a section designed to hook the reader. It is generally 25 percent of the story. Consider the length of your set-up compared to the middle and ending sections. You might want to time each scene. Is the ratio working? Then ask if the plot moves forward in a compelling way, holding the audience's attention. Mystery and uncertainty will effectively keep people glued to the presentation, but are there holes in the logic?

Read the first draft again and ask if your obligatory scene is positioned well in relation the rest of the story. I find it helpful to work backward from the obligatory scene to make sure it's set up in a logical way. You want early action to harness audience expectations for that scene. So, make sure that the story builds toward the inevitable moment for which everyone waits.

In regard to the drama's structure, pay close attention to exposition, which is the information that audiences need to understand the back story. You usually won't need much background information. However, biographical dramas often start in the middle of the story, so writers need to work out clever ways to include the back story without zapping forward motion.

As mentioned earlier, many good biographical dramas use opening titles to provide background information. In *A Very English Scandal* (2018), a film about British politician Jeremy Thorpe, a slide gives us this information: *Based on a true story, London 1965, House of Commons dining room.* Two middle-age men meet in the dining room. After some banter about opportunities for advancing political careers, they reveal that they are both attracted to men. This prepares the audience for the first flashback, which is presented with a slide saying: *Four years earlier.* Then we see the countryside where Jeremy Thorpe first met the young man who caused the central scandal of the film.

In *Trust* (2018), a biographical television series about billionaire John Paul Getty and his grandson's kidnapping, the writer used a slide to present crucial information: *The following is inspired by actual events.* The first image is of a young man running desperately through sunflowers. He looks as if he is running for his life. Then, abruptly, we see an expensive Hollywood party and the famous Hollywood sign in the background. Partygoers near a huge swimming pool sing Pink Floyd's "Money" as young, slim women play in the water. Expensive 1970s cars are parked all around. This image moves to a woman calling out desperately for "George." A man appears, whom we presume is George, in a drug-dazed state in one of the estate's many garages. Four women look through the windows of the garage as the obviously distressed George stabs himself with a barbeque fork. A slide then announces: *The House of Getty.*

Slides are also used in theater. One of Bertolt Brecht's biographical works, *The Life of Galileo (*1943), used placards held by the actor to introduce vital information, such as dates and a bit of history. This allowed Brecht to begin a scene without too much energy draining exposition.

Your Character's First Impact

Next, read the script and consider whether your character makes a great first impression. By that I don't mean, necessarily, a *positive* first impression; your lead character could be a despicable person. But your subject should have a *strong* first impact on the audience. Remember that biographical drama audiences have preconceptions about well-known subjects. So, make sure to give your character a powerful introduction. My audiences knew that Barassi was a famous motivator, so the first time I portrayed him on stage, I had him deliver a short version of a famous speech he delivered before a historic win against Collingwood (The Magpies).

The speech ended (with him shouting) as follows: "I want fried Magpie, fried Magpies what I want for my supper, and it will go beautifully with champagne!" My audiences would laugh and relax as they accepted my interpretation of their hero.

In the 2016 play *The Lehman Trilogy*, the opening image is of a modern glass office with scattered file boxes. When many people think of the collapse of Lehman Brothers, which precipitated the 2008 global financial crisis, many remember press images of the company's former employees leaving the building with file boxes of personal belongings. The script included these boxes as platforms for three actors to tell the story of the company's rise and fall. We first see one of the main characters, Henry Lehman, step onto a rotating glass box and onto a modern file box while wearing a three-piece, nineteenth-century suit. It is a vivid opening image. Immediately we feel in safe but interesting hands.

When and how will your audience first see your subject's character?

Review Each Character

After you've considered your main subject, look carefully at the other characters one at a time, making sure that their choices, actions, and reactions make sense in relation to who they are. Audiences need to understand more than the factual aspects of their lives; they need to know *why* the characters made their decisions. Is that coming through in your script in a compelling way?

Emotional Power

Review your script to make sure there is ongoing emotional power. For example, Napoleon and Josephine loved each other, but they also had affairs. Would showing those affairs intensify or distract from the emotional power? As you read, look for areas that might seem flat, boring, or shallow. Does the drama engage the audience emotionally? What is the moment-to-moment emotional experience? Can you fudge the facts, while still being ethical, to enhance the emotion?

A good way to strengthen emotional power is to intensify the rivalry between your subject and the antagonist. Do you see a way to ramp-up tension leading to the crisis? A good example of tension between a main character and an antagonist is in *The Assassination of Gianni Versace: American Crime Story* (2018). The writers included intercut scenes that show what the two men were doing in the hour before the assassination. As Versace enjoyed his morning, Cunanan was sweating, throwing up, and erratic. In later episodes, the writers presented flashbacks of the two men's childhoods. Versace's mother, after seeing one of the dresses designed by her young boy, encouraged him to create clothes for women, adding that he would have to work hard. By contrast, Cunanan's father repeatedly told him that he was special, even though he hadn't achieved anything.

Another example of how fictional antagonists can increase a biographical drama's emotional impact is found in *Judy* (2019). Hollywood movie star and singer Judy Garland asked two fans to take her to dinner. Unable to find anything open late, they took her to their simple flat and cooked a sloppy omelet. That she asked two strangers to share a meal displayed Judy's loneliness, the result of her broken relationships. When, at dinner, one of the fans revealed how his partner had been jailed for being gay, the scene showed her empathy. This exchange was designed to help audiences bond with Judy even though she behaved badly and let people down.

You can also increase the audience's emotional connection to your subject's job. For instance, imagine that your subject is investigative *New York Times* journalist Judith Miller, who spent time in jail for refusing to reveal a source. As you look at the scenes leading to her imprisonment, you could increase emotional impact by showing Miller tussling between her commitment to her source and her fear of going to jail. You could show her agony as she thinks about how jail will impact her family and her professional future. And you could reveal how her pride motivates her refusal to give in.

I wanted audiences to feel the enormous physical and mental pressure Barassi endured to become a top captain and coach, an ambition that led to his divorce and bankruptcy. In my rewrites, I focused on how to demonstrate this through images, such as having Barassi repeatedly practicing to become more proficient at the sport.

Consider Performability

Whereas fiction and nonfiction books need to be readable, all dramas for screen and stage must be performable. Your biographical drama script should suggest interesting opportunities for the director to stage the play or film the scenes, ways to illustrate your subject's life story and your thematic ambitions. Your job is not the director's, but you can help the director consider ways to portray the full potential of your script through exciting images and action.

In *A Beautiful Mind*, screenwriter Akiva Goldsman chose to

give the central character, John Nash, both visual as well as auditory hallucinations, even though Nash only suffered from auditory hallucinations.

Michael Frayn's play *Copenhagen* included a debate between two physicists about building the atomic bomb. Frayn had the characters argue as they walked in Copenhagen. The play's first director, Michael Blakemore, explained what the script suggested to him: "I felt that if we had the actors moving rather like particles within an atom, there would be times when this would be instructive and other times when as a metaphor it might be quite interesting" (Shephard-Barr, 2006).

As you review your script, consider how the director and actors will study it. Make sure that the script is conducive to actual production. In a biographical drama, the actor is a co-historian with you. He or she is keen to represent and perform your subject. Ask yourself:

1. Have I given my characters penetrating dialogue that reveals meaningful aspects of who they are?
2. Do all the scenes have a dramatic drive?
3. Do the characters sound true to their real personalities?

As mentioned before, dialogue in drama must have a compelling purpose. Directors and actors often use a device called "actioning" to verify that dialogue is powerful. In rehearsal, actors break down scenes and identify the underlying dramatic actions, typically expressed as transitive verbs (annoy, reassure, persuade, tempt, tame, uplift, etc.). Actors read the script and decide what the character wants or needs in the scene. Then, each time they say a line of dialogue, they focus on how the character *gets* what he or she wants.

This intense aspect of revision is designed to give purpose to every line of dialogue. Actors pencil in transitive verbs as they deliver a line. As an example, I have placed a verb (*in italics*) beside the character's name:

CLEOPATRA: (*admonishes*) Fool! (*enlightens*) Don't you see now that I could have poisoned you a hundred times had I been able to live without you?

NAPOLEAN: (*teaches*) Never interrupt your enemy when he is making a mistake.

Likewise, writers find it helpful to isolate tactics or motivations behind each line of dialogue. This can give writers better insight into where dialogue is powerful and where it needs to be tweaked. Revising with this approach might reveal where in the script your characters need to be more varied in their attempts to get what they want.

Here's an example of revision to improve word choice from a *Barassi* excerpt. This is a great technique to improve word choice. The following scene is set in 1950s Melbourne. Barassi is sixteen-years old and his mother, Elza, has just married Colin, who lives in Tasmania and they plan to leave Melbourne and move there. Norm is Barassi's father's former best friend who coaches at the Melbourne Football Club. Both Norm and Barassi need to persuade Elza to let her sixteen-year-old son stay in Melbourne in order for him to play for his deceased father's club. They are in a suburban street and Barassi is holding a football.

NORM: (*warns*) Tasmania will never release him to Melbourne. If he plays for them, he'll never be able to play for his father's club.

ELZA: (*worries*) But Ronny can't live on his own. (*justifies*) What with me working, he's been on his own too long.

BARASSI: (*appeases*) I don't mind living on my own.

NORM: (*suggests*) I've talked to Marj and we think Ron could move in with us.

ELZA: (*reprimands*) You've no room.

NORM: (*informs*) We'll build a bungalow out the back. Give the lad some privacy.

BARASSI: (*consoles*) Mum I'll visit you all the time.

COLIN: (*reassures*) And if the boy isn't any good, he can come live with us.

BARASSI: (*insults*) Thanks, Col.

COLIN: (*comforts obliviously*) That's alright boy. (*reassures*) You'll always be welcome at the Brewster home.

ELZA: (*shames*) You want to live away from me Ronny?

BARASSI: (*yields*) No, Mum I . . .

ELZA: (*confirms*) Good. Then it's settled. He finishes his schooling in Tasmania.

BARASSI: (*protests*) Mum!

ELZA: (*reinforces*) It's my final word.

Notice how the transitive verbs can help map the emotional progress of the scene. Confirm that the tactics used by characters to get what they want are varied and progressive. I find it helpful to read each line of dialogue out loud in the manner of the transitive verb to test that the tactic will work with the words. Reading out loud can confirm that the dialogue sounds realistic and compelling, and that the words fit with the characters' personalities during the era in which they lived.

After Elza's "final word," Norm persuaded the young Barassi to kick a football into a neighbor's bin at the end of the street. Barassi's kick was so powerful and precise that the ball landed in the bin. Then Norm asked him to kick the ball and to aim at the cat on another neighbor's lawn. After watching a powerful kick and hearing a cat squeal, Elza changed her mind. She realized that her son had a gift that would be wasted in Tasmania. So, look for ways that action can tell the story or persuade an antagonist.

Please note! Actors must find their own motivations, so *you should not leave the verbs in your script*, otherwise you will disrupt the creative process of the director and actors. This is just a revision exercise to potentially improve the dialogue's vivacity.

This approach also works well to test monologues. If each line has the same intention, for example to inform, then you may have to rewrite. Extended passages in the past tense can stifle energy. Perhaps you have too much exposition, with characters talking extensively about something that happened in the past. Biographical dramas thrive in the present.

The Process for Initial Readings

After you've revised the first draft with the criteria above in mind, the next step is to finalize a second draft so that it's ready for others to read. Now you wear your master architect's hat. I liken the second draft to finalizing a blueprint—fine-tuning the original sketches, adding the specific details, removing things that aren't helpful. The blueprint, or what some people prefer to call an artist's rendition, is what directors and actors will use to "construct" your biographical drama for stage or screen.

During this phase, I recommend that you print out the most recent version of the script. Looking at the printed script can help you see the big picture, like an actual blueprint rolled across an architect's long table. Having a physical copy of the script enables you to shuffle pages around while rewriting.

How to Share Your Work

When you have taken the second draft about as far as you can, then give it to two or three trusted and intelligent script-savvy people for feedback. Avoid giving it to family members, at least for now. It's best to share it with people who are familiar with reading scripts, people who can read it as a working document and who can give you meaningful, professional feedback. It can be helpful to give the script to some readers who know your subject well and some who know nothing about your subject. Give everyone time to read the script carefully and to prepare comments.

When you receive feedback, allow the comments to sit with

you for a while before you make another round of changes. You don't need to obey every suggestion, but you should take them to heart.

Initiate the First Reading

After you have made additional changes based on reader feedback, your script should be ready for the first public reading. Using actors at the theater or film company that commissioned you is ideal. If that's not possible, try to gather actors who support you. If you have the funds, pay them to do a sit-down reading, perhaps in a hall, a rented room, or in your home.

Send the script to the actors before they come to the first reading. I have found that only about one quarter of the actors read the script before the first reading, but the ones who do are often more in tune with the story. Have extra scripts available on the day of the reading just in case the actors forget to bring a copy.

Prior to the gathering, make sure the room is easy to get to by public transport or has good parking. It should be insulated from outside noise, be reasonably comfortable, and have a table for coffee, tea, and biscuits (cookies).

Once you have determined the location and time, you can send out invitations to friends and colleagues. Your group doesn't need to be large, but the people you invite should know that you'll be asking them for feedback. If possible, choose people who represent your target audience.

When all the readers have gathered around the table and when all your guests are seated, thank them for their help and describe the importance of the reading. Ask everyone to turn off their cellphones.

Do not muddy the process by talking too much about the script. You don't want to influence participants' views before it's read. It is vital for them to respond to the reading, not to your interpretation of the script.

If possible, have an actor, or perhaps a director (if you have one), read the stage or screen directions. This frees you up to listen, observe, and take notes. As you listen to the reading, mark your copy of the script when the actors stumble or fail to deliver your intentions. Do the same if your mind wanders at certain points during the reading. Jot down those moments in which you are not satisfied, even if it's a vague feeling that something is not quite working. You can figure out why later. In these cases, you could ask your participants to re-read the problematic scenes.

After the reading, take a break. Then let the actors and guests share their responses. Ask them to be specific. This is a perfect time to verify that you have not over-taxed the audience's comprehension. Did everyone follow the story? If not, where did they get lost? Encourage them to show you where in the script they had a problem or felt confused.

It is important for you to listen (humility!). Don't answer questions or defend yourself when they offer criticism. It is more important to write down the feedback, for your own benefit and as a way of showing how much you value the participation of those in attendance.

The Fine Art of Utilizing Feedback

Before you implement another round of changes to your script, take a break for a few days after the reading. Then, as my character

Barassi would say, "Get some guts!" Based on the feedback, have the bravery to cut or change scenes that aren't working. Sometimes your favorite scene is only *your* favorite, even though it fails to work for the audience. You don't want the audience to lose interest or start wondering what they are going to have for dinner as they watch *your* favorite scene!

How you deal with feedback is a key to a writer's success. On the one hand, you don't want to accept all advice. Counsel from experienced people isn't always best. So, you must deconstruct the feedback. It's your script. You've been working on it a lot longer than the theater or film workers. You've done the research and gained unique personal insights about the subject. Be grateful for the feedback, but only accept what you know will improve the work.

However, be careful to not allow your ego to get in the way. If someone has a good idea that will result in a better script, take it as a gift! You can't be lazy and survive in this business! You've come this far, so why not rewrite it when a change will significantly improve the outcome.

I recommend that you save all old drafts. Sometimes a revision doesn't work and you need to find another way to solve the problem. Persevere! Maybe return to the free writing that I described in the chapter on writing. Persistence will get you through.

The Rehearsal/Production Phase

The production phase is when directors and actors and producers and set designers move into action. Scripts are heavily scrutinized during the rehearsals. Directors and actors usually have strong preconceptions about biographical drama subjects, so you will need to confidently convey your intentions. You might have to explain your use of dramatic license. Be willing to amend the script when a director makes a suggestion, but don't concede to every idea. Sometimes actors and directors just need more time to find a solution. Playwrights generally have more power than screenwriters to insist on their ideas.

With biographical dramas, it's more likely that new information about your subject might come to light during production. Australian playwright and screenwriter David Williamson's subject, newspaper magnate Rupert Murdoch, kept hitting the headlines every time Williamson thought he had finished his 2013 biographical play *Rupert*. A frustrated Williamson said in *The Australian*, "I'd no sooner done the rewrite to cope with the marriage break-up than Rupert is caught on tape possibly contradicting what he told the Leveson inquiry" (Blundell, 2013).

However, at some point you must let your collaborators create the world that you've written. Constantly tweaking a script can upset actors and directors. Film and theater workers have long been working with your blueprint, so changing lines deep in the production phase can upset the creative process. Tom Stoppard (I think) said that writers never finish scripts; they just abandon them.

That said, many stage actors and directors are open to last minute changes, usually until about three weeks before opening night. Companies that are particularly playwright friendly will keep developing the play throughout the production. Plays, of course, can have several remounts. The acceptance of last-minute rewrites always depends on the actor's generosity.

Playing a haughty princess in *The Crown*, actor Helena

Bonham Carter, who played Princess Margaret, evoked the princess's unwillingness to oblige. Bonham Carter said: "A lot of the time, [screenwriter Peter] Morgan will send rewrites. Margaret's convenient because I can just say no. I can pull rank. It's the license to be powerful. 'Don't want any new lines now, mate. You should have given me them last week! Can't do'" (Van Arendonk, 2019).

By developing a good working relationship with actors and directors to shape the performance of a biographical drama, you, my dear writer, will have a deeply rewarding experience!

Epilogue

Our work as bio-dramatists is to transform a real person's life into a powerful, dramatic story. This is not easy because our subjects' lives are usually messy and unstructured. Writing biographical dramas has challenged me in ways I never anticipated. Being immersed in research while balancing biases, facts, and dramaturgical goals makes the craft of biographical drama writing an exhilarating adventure.

My final advice to you is to be wary of advice! Artists can deepen their knowledge through books like this one, but ultimately you will write your biographical drama your own way. Take what is useful from this book and ignore what isn't. My views about the biographical dramas mentioned in this book, including my own works, would no doubt spark debate. Moreover, writers are never in control of the responses to their works, just as we are not in control of what others think about our lives.

Bio-dramatists defy simplistic definitions. They can be many things: storytellers, restorers of reputations, vandals, gossipmongers, truth tellers, judges and jurists, apologists, opportunistic plagiarists, or perhaps lazy opportunists. We can also be miracle workers; or dare I say, gods, for we can bring to life someone who would otherwise be dead.

Writing any script is difficult, but when a writer sees an audience that has been deeply moved and changed by a biographical drama presented in a dramatically truthful way, there is no better feeling in the world.

I sincerely hope that, very soon, you will have this profound experience while sitting anonymously among people who are watching *your* biographical drama.

About the Author

Tee O'Neill is a recipient of the Edward Albee Award, the RE Ross Trust Playwright's Award, and the Siena College International Play Award. She earned an International Residency at the Royal Court Theatre in London, as well as a Winston Churchill Fellowship. She has been nominated for the Griffin Award, the Louis Esson Prize, and the Australian Writer's Guild Award. She has also been nominated for the WA and NSW Premier's Award, the Patrick White Play Award (twice), the Wal Cherry Award, and Corcadorca Play of the Year in Ireland. Dr. O'Neill has received writing grants from the Australia Council, Arts Victoria, the Sidney Myer Fund, and the Ian Potter Foundation.

Dr. O'Neill's professional involvement includes working as an Affiliate Writer for the Melbourne Theatre Company. Her works have been produced and commissioned by the Sydney Theatre Company, MTC, Playbox and Theatre@Risk, and the New York University School of TISCH.

Her plays include *Barassi: The Stage Show* (Athenaeum Theatre, Arts Centre, and regional tour); *Best Possible World* (Sydney, Dublin, and Melbourne); *The Dogs Play* (Playbox Theatre and theaters worldwide); *The Last Antigone* (Trinity College Dublin and Otago University in New Zealand); *Homage to Rembrandt* (Melbourne Theatre Company); *Stalking Matilda*; *The Wall Project*; and *Requiem for the Twentieth Century* (Theatre@Risk). Her Edward Albee Award-winning *GR8Skin* opened the inaugural WITS conference in Sydney in 2016.

Academically, Dr. O'Neill has been a lecturer in scriptwriting and dramatic structure for fifteen years, including three years at the New York University School of TISCH. In 2007, she was writer in residence at New York's Siena College. In 2008 she was the William Evans Fellow in Playwriting at Otago University in New Zealand, and in 2009 she was Visiting Creative Writing Fellow for the National University of Singapore. In 2010 to 2013, she worked as a theater writing coordinator for Melbourne University. She held master classes in playwriting for theater students at the University of New England in 2016. Her latest play, *Yellingbo*, was performed at La Mama in 2021. Dr. O'Neill's site-specific biographical drama on the 1930's horticulturist Edna Walling had its fifth return season in one of Walling's most famous gardens in November 2024.

Dr. O'Neill holds a master's degree in playwriting from the University of Birmingham and a PhD in biographical scriptwriting. She has written a series of novels about the biographical playwright detective Tilda Ransome in *The Tilda Ransome Series*.

Tee lives on a farm in the Yarra Valley of Australia with five cows, five horses, two dogs, and one husband.

For more about Dr. O'Neill, visit: www.teeoneill.com.

Acknowledgements

Books are written alone, but they are shaped by a community. I was blessed to have help on this long, circuitous road to a final draft.

I would love to thank Professor Susan Thomas who guided me so carefully and patiently as supervisor of my PhD thesis, from which this book is adapted. Also, love and thanks to my clever friend and best early reader, Catriona Mitchell, and to another great friend, Karen Berger, who always scoops me up when I'm a puddle on the floor.

I'm honored to thank the eleven playwrights and screenwriters from around the globe who gave me the opportunity to interview them. Peter Arnott, Patricia Cornelius, Motti Lerner, Kenneth Lin, Rebecca Miller, Willie Russell, José Rivera, Robert Reid, Nick Stimson, Polly Teale, and Roy Williams were open and generous when I asked about the creative processes they use when writing biographical scripts. An arts journalist once commented to me that playwrights are among the best people. I agree.

A big thanks to Janelle Shields who got me through that difficult process of adapting an academic thesis into the first draft of this book. A feeling of deep appreciation goes to my editor, Glenn McMahan, who helped shape that draft into this book, and for his unfailing energy and belief in this project. I'm also grateful for my hard-working transcribers, Kiem-Ai Nguyen and Ingrid Jager, for faithfully and accurately transcribing the interviews.

A huge amount of insight about the power of biographical performance came during the rehearsal and performance of my play *Barassi*. I was blessed by my director, Terence O'Connell, and lead actors Steve Bastoni and Chris O'Connell, who played Barassi with the ferocity and authenticity of the real legend. My eternal gratitude goes to my three fictional, footy, fanatic narrators Jane Clifton, Odette Joannides, and Carmelina di Guglielo who helped produce a better script.

Finally, I must thank my partner Al, who encourages and supports and never doubts. His positivity is blessedly infectious (though I wish he'd stop whistling).

Cited Works

(Excluding Personal Interviews)

Bennett, A. *The Habit of Art*. London: Faber and Faber, 1991.

Bentley, Eric. *Bentley on Brecht*. North Western University Press, 1966.

Brenton, H. *Never So Good*. London: Nick Hern Books, 2008.

Brown, P. "Amadeus and Mozart: Setting the Record Straight." *The American Scholar* 61, no. 1, 1992.

Canton, U. *Biographical Theatre: Re-Presenting Real People?* London: Palgrave MacMillan, 2011.

Cantrell, T. and Luckhurst, M (eds). *Playing for Real*. London: Palgrave MacMillan, 2010.

Cheeseman, Peter. Cited in "Verbatim Theatre: Oral History and Documentary Techniques" by Derek Paget. Cambridge.org 3, Issue 12, 1987.

Coveny, M. "Pam Gems: Playwright Celebrated for Her Biographical Works which Explored Their Subject's Dark Sides." *The Independent*, May 18, 2011, http://www.independent.co.uk/news/obituaries/ pam-gems-playwright-celebrated-for-her-biographical-works-which-explored-their-subjectsrsquo-dark-2285338.html.

Edgar, D. "In Defense of Evil." *The Guardian*, April 30, 2000, https:// www.theguardian.com/theobserver/2000/apr/30/featuresreview. review2.

Edgar, D. *How Plays Work*, London: Nick Hern Books, 2009.

Egri, L. *The Art of Dramatic Writing*. New York: Simon and Schuster, 1946.

Farley, C.J., "Tony Kushner Fires Back at Congressman's 'Lincoln' Criticism." *The Wall Street Journal*, February 8, 2013, https://blogs.wsj.com/speakeasy/2013/02/08/tony-kushner-fires-back-at-congressmans-lincoln-criticism/.

Frayn, Michael. *Michael Frayn Plays 4*. London: Bloomsbury, 2010.

Grace, S. and Wasserman, J. (eds). *Theatre and Autobiography*. Vancouver: Talon Books, 2006.

Hare, D. *The Blue Touch Papers*. London: Faber and Faber, 2015.

Hattaway, Michael. *The Cambridge Companion to Shakespeare's History Plays*. Cambridge: Cambridge University Press, 2003.

Kendall, P.M. *Richard the Third*. New York: W.W. Norton and Company, 1955.

King, Stephen. *On Writing: A Memoir of the Craft*. New York: Scribner, 2000.

Kushner, T. *Angels in America: A Gay Fantasia on National Themes*. New York: Bloomsbury, 1993.

Lalor, P. *Barassi: The Biography*. Allen & Unwin, 2010.

Lamott, Anne. *Bird by Bird: Some Instructions on Writing and Life*. New York: Anchor Books, 1995.

Lawrence, B. "An audience with Jimmy Savile." *The Telegraph*, June 12, 2015, http://www.telegraph.co.uk/culture/theatre/theatre-reviews/11668043/An-Audience-with-Jimmy-Savile-Park-Theatre-review-merely-depressing.html.

Lower, Cheryl and Palmer, R. Barton. *Joseph L. Mankiewicz: Critical Essays with an Annotated Bibliography and a Filmography.* London: McFarland, 2001.

Mamet, David. *Three Uses of the Knife.* New York: Vintage Books, 1998.

McDonald, Dani. "Kiwi Writer Anthony McCarten on Queen, the Popes, John Lennon and Weed," Stuff (website), June 16, 2017, https://www.stuff.co.nz/entertainment/stage-and-theatre/93771679/kiwi-writer-anthony-mccarten-on-queen-the-popes-john-lennon-and-weed.

McKee, R. *Story: Substance, Structure, Style and the Principles of Screenwriting.* London: Methuen, 1999.

Miller, Arthur. *Timebends: A Life.* London: Bloomsbury, 1995.

Morgan, Peter. "Peter Morgan on Frost/Nixon by David Calhoun." TimeOut (website), 2009, https://www.timeout.com/london/film/peter-morgan-on-frost-nixon-1.

Nadel, I. *Tom Stoppard, A Life.* New York: Palgrave McMillian, 2002.

Ngangura, Tari. "Why It Is Nearly Impossible to Write a Good Biopic." Vice (website), August 23, 2017.

Parks, S. L. *The America Play and other Works.* New York: Theater Communications Group, 1995.

Paulin, T. "Frayn and Heisenberg." *The Guardian*, March 27, 2002, https://www.theguardian.com/theguardian/2002/mar/27/guardianletters.

Pinter, Harold. Royal Court Theatre lecture, 1998.

Rokem, F. *Performing History: Theatrical Representations of the Past in Contemporary Theatre.* Iowa City: University of Iowa Press, 2000.

Rosenthal, Daniel (ed.). *Dramatic Exchanges: The Lives and Letters of the National Theatre.* London: Profile Books, 2019.

Sacks, Oliver. "Pinter, the Creative Process and Refusing a Play." Web of Stories (website), viewed November 12, 2013, webofstories.com/play/oliver.sacks/175.

Script. "Adapting 'A Beautiful Mind': Screenwriter Akiva Goldsman." December 19, 2012.

Shephard-Barr, Kirsten. *Science on Stage: From Doctor Faustus to Copenhagen.* Princeton: Princeton University Press, 2006.

Smiley, S. *Playwriting: The Structure of Action.* London: Yale University Press, 2005.

Stanislavski, C. *An Actor Prepares.* Routledge, New York: Theatre Arts Book, 1936.

Stephenson, H. and Langridge, N. *Rage and Reason: Women Playwrights on Playwriting.* London: Methuen Drama, 1997.

Stoppard, Tom. "Ideas at the House: Tom Stoppard—In Conversation with Jonathon Biggins." YouTube (website), Sydney Opera House Talks and Ideas, October 9, 2013, https://www.youtube.com/watch?v=AxyNXciuby4.

VanArendonk, Kathryn. Vulture (website). October 28, 2019.

Wallenberg, Christopher. "Rothko's Paintings Colored Dramatist's 'Red.'" *Boston Globe*, January 7, 2012.

Wright, D. "Q & A with 'I am My Own Wife' Playwright Doug Wright." *The Denver Post*, September 5.

Zinsser, William. *On Writing Well: The Classic Guide to Writing Non-Fiction.* New York: HarperResource Quill edition, 2001.